Andorra

The imaginary republic of Andorra is invaded by the totalitarian forces of 'The Blacks'. The Andorrans capitulate to the anti-semitism of the aggressor and betray Andri, the foundling son of the local school-master, who has already become an outcast in their eyes. Ironically it turns out that the victim was not a Jew at all.

This translation of *Andorra* was produced at the National Theatre in January, 1964.

'Max Frisch has written a supremely important play, one of the most important to be written in the German language since 1945'.   *Encounter*

The photograph on the front cover is of the 1964 National Theatre production of Andorra *at the old Vic and is reproduced by courtesy of Lewis Morley Studios. The photograph of Max Frisch on the back is reproduced by courtesy of Suhrkamp Verlag, Frankfurt.*

Max Frisch

ANDORRA

translated by
MICHAEL BULLOCK

METHUEN · LONDON

A Methuen Paperback

Paperback edition first published in Great Britain
by Methuen & Co. Ltd
in 1964
Reprinted 1968, 1970, 1973 and 1979
Reprinted 1983 by Methuen London Ltd
This translation © 1962 and 1964 by Michael Bullock;
original work published under the title of
ANDORRA
© 1961 by Suhrkamp Verlag, Frankfurt am Main
ISBN 0 413 30510 4

Reproduced, printed and bound in Great Britain by
Richard Clay (The Chaucer Press) Ltd, Bungay, Suffolk

All enquires concerning the rights for
professional or amateur stage production
should be directed to the
International Copyright Bureau Ltd
26 Charing Cross Road, London WC2

Andorra

A PLAY IN TWELVE SCENES

Andorra. The Andorra of this play has nothing to do with the real small state of this name, nor does it stand for another real small state; Andorra is the name of a model.

Names. The following names have the stress on the final syllable: Barblín, Andrí, Pradér, Ferrér, Fedrí. In the name Peider the stress falls on the first syllable.

Costumes. Costumes should not be traditional. The Andorrans wear modern ready-made clothes; it will be sufficient if their hats are peculiar to them, and they almost always wear hats. An exception is the Doctor, whose hat is in keeping with international fashion. Andri wears blue jeans. Barblin wears a ready-made costume, even when taking part in the procession, but over it she wears a shawl decorated with Andorran embroidery. All the men wear white shirts and nobody wears a tie, with the exception once more of the Doctor. Unlike all the others, the Señora is smartly, but unostentatiously, dressed. The uniform of the Andorran soldiers is olive-grey. Any resemblance to uniforms of the past is to be avoided in the uniform of the Blacks.

Types. Some of the parts might lead to caricature. This should under all circumstances be avoided. It is enough that they are types. They should be played in such a way that the spectator at first likes, or at least tolerates, them, since they all appear innocuous, and that he always sees them in their true light rather too late, as in real life.

Setting. The basic setting for the whole play is the square in Andorra. This should be a square typical of any southern country, not picturesque, bare, white with a few touches of colour (shutters, Shell posters etc.) beneath a gloomy blue sky. The stage should be as empty as possible. A vista at the back indicates how Andorra is to be imagined; nothing but what the actors require should be present in the acting-area. All those scenes that do not take place in the square are to be set in front of it. No curtain between scenes, only the displacement of the light onto the forestage. No anti-illusionism need be demonstrated, but the spectator should be continuously reminded that a model is being shown, as in fact is always the case in the theatre.

First performed on 2 November 1961 at the Schauspiel-
haus, Zürich, and directed by Kurt Hirschfeld.

Characters

Speaking
ANDRI
BARBLIN
THE TEACHER
THE MOTHER
THE SEÑORA
THE PRIEST
THE SOLDIER
THE INNKEEPER
THE CARPENTER
THE DOCTOR
THE JOURNEYMAN
THE SOMEBODY

Silent
AN IDIOT
THE SOLDIERS IN BLACK UNIFORMS
THE JEW DETECTOR
THE ANDORRAN PEOPLE

*Outside an Andorran house. Barblin is whitewashing the
high, narrow wall with a brush on a long stick. An Andorran
soldier in olive-grey is leaning against the wall.*

BARBLIN If you could take your eyes off my legs for a minute you
could see what I'm doing. I'm whitewashing. Because
tomorrow is St George's Day, in case you've forgotten.
I'm whitewashing my father's house. And what do you
soldiers do? You just hang about the streets with your
thumbs in your belts, squinting into our blouses when
we bend down.
The Soldier laughs.
Anyway, I'm engaged.

SOLDIER Engaged!

BARBLIN What are you laughing at?

SOLDIER Is he pigeon-chested?

BARBLIN Why should he be?

SOLDIER Because you never let us see him.

BARBLIN Leave me alone!

SOLDIER Or flat-footed?

BARBLIN Why should he be flat-footed?

SOLDIER Anyhow, he doesn't dance with you.
Barblin whitewashes.
Perhaps he's an angel!
The Soldier laughs.
That's why I've never seen him.

BARBLIN I'm engaged!

SOLDIER Well, I don't see any ring.

BARBLIN I'm engaged.
She dips the brush in the bucket.
And anyway – I don't like you.
*On the forestage right stands a juke box, by which – as
Barblin whitewashes – there appear the Carpenter, a
corpulent man, and behind him Andri as a kitchen-boy.*

CARPENTER Where's my stick?

ANDRI Here, sir.

CARPENTER A bloody nuisance, these tips all the time. No sooner have you taken your hand out of your pocket –

Andri gives him his stick and receives a tip which he drops into the juke box so that music starts up, while the Carpenter walks across the front of the stage, forcing Barblin to move her bucket out of his way. Andri dries a plate, moving in time to the music, and then goes out as the music stops.

BARBLIN Are you still there?

SOLDIER I'm on leave.

BARBLIN What else do you want to know?

SOLDIER Who is your fiancé supposed to be?

Barblin whitewashes.

They're all whitewashing their father's houses, because tomorrow is St George's Day, and the coal-sack is tearing around on his bicycle. Whitewash, you virgins, whitewash your father's houses, so that we have a white Andorra, you virgins, a snow-white Andorra!

BARBLIN The coal-sack – who on earth is that?

SOLDIER Are you a virgin?

The Soldier laughs.

So you don't like me.

BARBLIN No.

SOLDIER A lot of women have told me that, but I've had them just the same, if I liked their legs and their hair.

Barblin puts out her tongue at him.

And their red tongue too!

The Soldier takes out a cigarette and looks up at the house.

Which is your room?

Enter a Priest pushing a bicycle.

PRIEST That's how I like to see it, Barblin, that's how I like to see it. We shall have a white Andorra, you virgins, a snow-white Andorra, so long as there isn't a cloudburst during the night.

The Soldier laughs.

Is your father at home?

SOLDIER So long as there isn't a cloudburst during the night! The fact is, his church isn't as white as he pretends, we know that now; his church is also only made of earth, and the earth is red, and when there's a cloudburst it washes off the whitewash and leaves a mess as if a pig had been slaughtered on it, and there's nothing left of your snow-white church.

The Soldier stretches out his hand to see if it is raining.

So long as there isn't a cloudburst during the night!

The Soldier laughs and strolls away.

PRIEST What was he doing here?

BARBLIN Is it true, Father, what people say? They'll attack us, the Blacks across the frontier, because they're jealous of our white houses. Early one morning they'll come with a thousand black tanks, and they'll roll in all directions over our fields, and they'll drop from the sky with parachutes like grey locusts.

PRIEST Who says that?

BARBLIN Peider, the soldier.

Barblin dips her brush in the bucket.

Father isn't at home.

PRIEST I might have guessed.

Why has he been drinking so much lately? And then he swears at everyone. He forgets who he is. Why does he always talk such rubbish?

BARBLIN I don't know what Father says in the inn.

PRIEST He sees ghosts. Wasn't everyone in this country horri-fied about the Blacks across the frontier when they be-haved like Herod during the Massacre of the Innocents? Didn't they collect clothes for the refugees? Now he's saying we're no better than the Blacks. Why does he keep saying that all the time? People take offence and I'm not surprised. A teacher shouldn't talk like that. And why does he believe every rumour that gets about in the inn?

Pause.

Nobody is persecuting your Andri –

Barblin stops and listens.

– nobody has yet hurt a hair of your Andri's head.

Barblin goes on whitewashing.

I see you take your work seriously, you're not a child
any more, you work like a grown-up girl.

BARBLIN I'm nineteen.

PRIEST And not engaged yet?

Barblin says nothing.

I hope that Peider doesn't have any luck with you.

BARBLIN No.

PRIEST He has dirty eyes.

Pause.

Did he frighten you? To make himself important. Why
should they attack us? Our valleys are narrow, our fields
are stony and steep, our olives are no juicier than else-
where. What should they want from us? Anyone who
wants our rye must reap it with the sickle, must bend
down and cut it step by step. Andorra is a beautiful country, but a poor country. A peaceful country, a weak
country – a pious country, so long as we fear God, and
we do fear Him, my child, don't we?

BARBLIN And suppose they come all the same?

A vesper bell, brief and monotonous.

PRIEST We shall see one another tomorrow, Barblin. Tell your
father St George doesn't want to see him drunk.

The Priest mounts his bicycle.

On second thoughts, don't tell him anything, it will only
irritate him, but keep an eye on him.

The Priest rides silently away.

BARBLIN And suppose they come all the same, Father?

*Front stage, right, by the juke box. The Somebody appears
with Andri behind him as a kitchen-boy.*

SOMEBODY Where's my hat?

ANDRI Here, sir.

SOMEBODY A heavy evening, I think there's a storm in the air . . .

*Andri gives him his hat and receives a tip, which he drops
into the juke box; he doesn't press the button, however, but
only whistles and studies the record selector, while the Somebody walks across the front of the stage and comes to a stop
before Barblin, who is whitewashing and hasn't noticed that
the Priest has cycled away.*

BARBLIN Is it true, Father, what people say? They say: When the Blacks come everyone who is a Jew will be taken away. He will be tied to a stake, they say, and shot in the back of the neck. Is that true or is it a rumour? And if he has a sweetheart she will have her head shaved, they say, like a mangy dog.

SOMEBODY That's a nice way to talk!

BARBLIN *turns round and starts with fright.*

SOMEBODY Good evening.

BARBLIN Good evening.

SOMEBODY A fine evening today.

BARBLIN *takes the bucket.*

SOMEBODY But heavy.

BARBLIN Yes.

SOMEBODY There's something in the air.

BARBLIN What do you mean by that?

SOMEBODY A storm. Everything is waiting for wind, the leaves and the dust and the curtains. And yet I can't see a cloud in the sky, but you can feel it. Such a hot stillness. The gnats can feel it too. Such a dry and stagnant heat. I think there's a storm in the air, a violent storm, it will do the land good . . .
Barblin goes indoors, the Somebody saunters on, Andri sets the juke-box going, the same record as before, and leaves drying a plate. The square of Andorra is seen. The Carpenter and the Teacher are sitting outside the inn. The music has stopped.

TEACHER Prader, it's my son I'm talking about.

CARPENTER I said, fifty pounds.

TEACHER My foster-son, I mean.

CARPENTER I still say, fifty pounds.
The Carpenter bangs on the table with a coin.
I must go.
The Carpenter bangs again.
Why does he want to be a carpenter of all things? It isn't easy to become a carpenter, you know, if it's not in your blood. And how could it be in his blood? You know what I mean. Why doesn't he become a stockbroker?

Why don't you put him on the Stock Exchange? You know what I mean . . .

TEACHER Prader, how did that stake get there?

CARPENTER What are you talking about?

TEACHER Look, there!

CARPENTER Are you feeling all right?

TEACHER I'm talking about a stake!

CARPENTER I can't see any stake.

TEACHER There!

The Carpenter has to turn round.

Is that a stake or isn't it?

CARPENTER Why shouldn't it be a stake?

TEACHER It wasn't there yesterday.

The Carpenter laughs.

Don't laugh, Prader, you know exactly what I mean.

CARPENTER You're seeing ghosts.

TEACHER What's it there for?

CARPENTER *bangs on the table with a coin.*

TEACHER I'm not drunk. I can see it, you can all see it.

CARPENTER I must go.

The Carpenter throws a coin on the table and stands up.

I've told you: Fifty pounds.

TEACHER Is that your last word?

CARPENTER My name is Prader.

TEACHER Fifty pounds?

CARPENTER I don't haggle.

TEACHER Oh no, you're above that sort of thing, we all know that . . . Prader, that's extortion, fifty pounds for a carpenter's apprenticeship, that's extortion. It's ridiculous, Prader, and you know it. I'm just an ordinary schoolmaster, living on a schoolmaster's salary, not a master carpenter – I haven't got fifty pounds, quite simply, I haven't got it!

CARPENTER Then there's no more to be said.

TEACHER Look, Prader –

CARPENTER I said, fifty pounds.

The Carpenter goes.

TEACHER Some day I'll tell them the truth – the bastards! I'll make

them see themselves as they really are, that'll wipe the
grins off their faces.

Enter the Innkeeper.

INNKEEPER What's the matter?

TEACHER I need a brandy.

INNKEEPER Trouble?

TEACHER Fifty pounds for a carpenter's apprenticeship!

INNKEEPER I heard him.

TEACHER I shall scrape it together.

The Teacher laughs.

If it isn't in your blood!

The Innkeeper wipes the table with a cloth.

They'll find out what their own blood is like.

INNKEEPER It's no good getting angry with your own people, it up-
sets you and doesn't change them. Of course it's extortion! The Andorrans are easy-going people, but, as I've
always said, when it's a question of money, they're like
the Jews.

The Innkeeper turns to go.

TEACHER How do you know what a Jew is like?

INNKEEPER Listen –

TEACHER How do you know?

INNKEEPER – I have nothing against your Andri. What do you think
I am? Otherwise I shouldn't have taken him on as a
kitchen-boy. What are you looking at me like that for?
Anyone will bear me out. Haven't I always said, Andri
is an exception?

TEACHER I'm not going to discuss it!

INNKEEPER A real exception –

The tolling of bells.

TEACHER Who put that stake there?

INNKEEPER What stake?

TEACHER I'm not always drunk, as the Reverend Father thinks.
A stake is a stake. Somebody put it there. It wasn't there
yesterday. A stake doesn't just grow up out of the ground,
does it?

INNKEEPER I don't know.

TEACHER What's it there for?

INNKEEPER I don't know, perhaps the surveyor's department, something to do with the roads perhaps, they've got to do something with the taxes, maybe a by-pass, you never know, maybe the drains –

TEACHER Maybe.

INNKEEPER Or the telephone –

TEACHER And maybe not.

INNKEEPER What's eating you?

TEACHER And what's the rope for?

INNKEEPER How should I know?

TEACHER I'm not mad, I'm not seeing ghosts, what I see is a stake that could be used for all sorts of things –

INNKEEPER What of it?

The Innkeeper goes into the inn. The Teacher is alone. More pealing of bells. The Priest hurries across the square in a chasuble followed by the little servers, whose censers leave a powerful smell of incense behind. The Innkeeper comes with the brandy.

INNKEEPER He wants fifty pounds, does he?

TEACHER I shall scrape it together.

INNKEEPER How?

TEACHER Somehow.

The Teacher drinks the brandy.

Sell land.

The Innkeeper sits down with the Teacher.

Somehow . . .

INNKEEPER How much land have you?

TEACHER Why?

INNKEEPER I'm always ready to buy land. If it's not too expensive! I mean, if you've got to raise money.

Noise outside the inn.

I'm coming!

The Innkeeper seizes the Teacher's arm.

Think it over, Can, in peace and quiet, but I can't pay more than fifty pounds –

The Innkeeper goes.

TEACHER 'The Andorrans are easy-going people, but when it's a question of money they're like the Jews.'

The Teacher puts the empty glass to his lips again, while Barblin, dressed for the procession, appears beside him.

BARBLIN Father!

TEACHER Why aren't you in the procession?

BARBLIN Father, you promised not to drink on St George's Day –

TEACHER *lays a coin on the table.*

BARBLIN They're coming past here.

TEACHER Fifty pounds for a carpenter's apprenticeship!

Now loud, high-pitched singing is heard, and the ringing of bells. The procession passes in the background. Barblin kneels down, the Teacher remains seated. People have gathered in the square. They all kneel down and above the heads of the kneeling people appear flags; the Virgin Mary is carried past accompanied by fixed bayonets. All cross themselves; the Teacher stands up and goes into the inn. The procession is slow and long and beautiful; the high-pitched singing is lost in the distance, the ringing of bells remains. Andri comes out of the inn, while the people in the square join the end of the procession; he stands on one side and whispers:

ANDRI Barblin!

BARBLIN *crosses herself.*

ANDRI Can't you hear me?

BARBLIN *stands up.*

ANDRI Barblin?

BARBLIN What is it?

ANDRI I'm going to be a carpenter!

Barblin tags on to the end of the procession; Andri is left alone.

The sun is shining green in the trees today. Today the bells are ringing for me too.

He takes off his apron.

I shall always remember this happiness. And yet I'm only taking off my apron. It's so quiet. I should like to throw my name in the air like a cap, and yet I'm only standing here rolling up my apron. This is happiness. I shall never forget the way I stood here today . . .

Uproar from the inn.

Barblin, we shall marry!
Andri goes.

INNKEEPER Get out! He's completely canned, then he always talks
such rubbish. Get out!
The Soldier staggers out with the drum.
You're not having another drop.

SOLDIER I'm a soldier.

INNKEEPER We can see that.

SOLDIER My name is Peider.

INNKEEPER We know that.

SOLDIER Well then.

INNKEEPER Stop making such a row!

SOLDIER Where is she?

INNKEEPER There's no sense in it, Peider. If a girl's willing she's
willing, if she isn't, she isn't. Shut up. Put your drum-
sticks away! You're tight. Think of the reputation of the
Army!
The Innkeeper goes back inside the inn.

SOLDIER Gutless bastards! They're not worth my fighting for. But
I shall fight. Don't you worry. To the last man, don't you
worry, rather dead than a slave, so I'm telling you: Watch
out – I'm a soldier and I've got my eye on her . . .
Enter Andri, putting on his jacket.
Where is she?

ANDRI Who?

SOLDIER Your sister.

ANDRI I haven't got a sister.

SOLDIER I said: Where is she?

ANDRI Why?

SOLDIER I'm off duty and I fancy her, that's why . . .
*Andri has put on his jacket and tries to walk on; the Soldier
sticks out his leg so that Andri trips up; the Soldier laughs.*
A soldier isn't a scarecrow. Got that? Walking past as if
I wasn't here. I'm a soldier, and you're a Jew.
Andri stands up without speaking.
You are a Jew, aren't you?
Andri says nothing.
But you're lucky, damned lucky, not every Jew is a

lucky as you are – you've got the chance to make yourself popular.
Andri brushes the dust from his trousers.
Did you hear what I said? I said you can make yourself
popular.

ANDRI Who with?

SOLDIER With the Army.

ANDRI You stink.

SOLDIER What did you say?

ANDRI Nothing. Nothing.

SOLDIER I stink?

ANDRI At seven paces and against the wind.

SOLDIER Take care what you say.
The Soldier tries to smell his own breath.
I can't smell anything.
Andri laughs.
It's no laughing matter being a Jew, it's no laughing
matter, a Jew has to make himself popular.

ANDRI Why?

SOLDIER *bawls:*
'When a man's in love,
And when a man's a soldier,
It's on the floor
And shut the door
And take your knickers off, girl – '
Stop staring at me as if you were a gentleman!
'When a man's in love,
And when a man's a soldier.'

ANDRI Can I go now?

SOLDIER Gentleman!

ANDRI I'm not a gentleman.

SOLDIER All right, then kitchen-boy.

ANDRI Ex-kitchen boy.

SOLDIER They wouldn't have your sort in the Army.

ANDRI Do you know what that is?

SOLDIER Money?

ANDRI My wages. I'm going to be a carpenter now.

SOLDIER Doesn't it make you sick!

ANDRI What do you mean?

SOLDIER I said, doesn't it make you sick.
The Soldier knocks the money out of his hand and laughs.
There!
Andri stares at the Soldier.
You Jews think of nothing but money all the time.
Andri controls himself with difficulty, then bends down and picks up the money from the pavement.
So you don't want to make yourself popular?

ANDRI No.

SOLDIER You're sure?

ANDRI Yes.

SOLDIER And we're supposed to fight for people like you? To the last man – do you know what that means, one battalion against twelve battalions, that's how it works out, rather dead than a slave, that's for sure, but not for you!

ANDRI What's for sure?

SOLDIER Andorrans aren't cowards. Let them come with their parachutes like the locusts from the sky, they won't get through, as true as my name is Peider, not past me. That's for sure. Not past me. They'll get the shock of their lives.

ANDRI Who will get the shock of their lives?

SOLDIER Not past me.
Enter an Idiot who can only grin and nod.
Did you hear that? He thinks we're scared. Because he's scared himself! We shan't fight to the last man, he says, we shan't die because we're outnumbered, we shall put our tails between our legs, we'll be in a blue funk, he dares to say that to my face, to the Army's face!

ANDRI I didn't say a word.

SOLDIER I ask you: Did you hear him?

IDIOT *nods and grins.*

SOLDIER An Andorran isn't scared!

ANDRI You've said that already.

SOLDIER But you're scared!

ANDRI *says nothing.*

SOLDIER Because you're a coward.

ANDRI Why am I a coward?

SOLDIER Because you're a Jew.

IDIOT *grins and nods.*

SOLDIER All right, now I'm going . . .

ANDRI You leave Barblin alone!

SOLDIER What red ears he's got!

ANDRI Barblin is my fiancée.

SOLDIER *laughs.*

ANDRI That's true.

SOLDIER *bawls*:

> 'It's on the floor
> And shut the door – '

ANDRI Go to hell!

SOLDIER Fiancée, he said!

ANDRI Barblin will turn her back on you.

SOLDIER Then I'll take her from behind!

ANDRI You're a pig.

SOLDIER What did you say?

ANDRI I said you're a pig.

SOLDIER Say that again. He's trembling! Say that again. But loudly, so the whole square can hear. Say that again.
Andri goes.
What did he say?

IDIOT *grins and nods.*

SOLDIER A pig? I'm a pig?

IDIOT *grins and nods.*

SOLDIER He's not making himself popular with me . . .

FORESTAGE

The Innkeeper, now without his apron, enters the witness-box

INNKEEPER I admit that we were all wrong over this business. At the time. Naturally I believed what everyone believed at the time. He believed it himself right up to the last minute. A Jewish kid our teacher saved from the Blacks across the frontier, that's what everybody thought, and we all thought it was marvellous the way the teacher looked after him like his own son. Anyhow, I thought it was marvellous. Did I tie him to the stake? None of us could have known that Andri really was his son, our teacher's son. When he was my kitchen-boy, did I treat him badly? It wasn't my fault that things turned out as they did. That's all I can say about the business after all this time. It wasn't my fault.

2

Andri and Barblin on the threshold outside Barblin's room.

BARBLIN Andri, are you asleep?

ANDRI No.

BARBLIN Why don't you give me a kiss?

ANDRI I'm awake, Barblin, I'm thinking.

BARBLIN All night long.

ANDRI Is it true what they say?
Barblin, who has been lying with her head in his lap, now sits up and undoes her hair.
Do you think they're right?

BARBLIN Don't start that again!

ANDRI Perhaps they're right.
Barblin busies herself with her hair.
Perhaps they're right.

BARBLIN You've made me all rumpled.

ANDRI They say my kind have no feelings.

BARBLIN Who says that?

ANDRI Lots of people.

BARBLIN Just look at my blouse!

ANDRI Everybody.

BARBLIN Shall I take it off?
Barblin takes off her blouse.

ANDRI They say my kind are lecherous, but heartless, you know –

BARBLIN Andri, you think too much!
Barblin lies down with her head in his lap again.

ANDRI I love your hair, your red hair, it's light, warm, it tastes

bitter, Barblin, I shall die if I lose it.
Andri kisses her hair.
You ought to be asleep.

BARBLIN *listens.*

ANDRI What was that?

BARBLIN The cat.

ANDRI *listens.*

BARBLIN I saw it.

ANDRI Was that the cat?

BARBLIN They're all asleep . . .
Barblin lays her head in his lap again.
Kiss me!

ANDRI *laughs.*

BARBLIN What are you laughing at?

ANDRI I ought to be grateful!

BARBLIN I don't know what you're talking about.

ANDRI Your father. He saved my life, he would think me very
ungrateful if I seduced his daughter. I'm laughing, but
it's no laughing matter always having to be grateful to
people for being alive.
Pause.
Perhaps that's why I'm not cheerful.

BARBLIN *kisses him.*

ANDRI Are you quite sure you want me, Barblin?

BARBLIN Why do you keep asking me that?

ANDRI The others are more fun.

BARBLIN The others!

ANDRI Perhaps they're right. Perhaps I am a coward, otherwise
I should go to your father and tell him we're engaged.
Do you think I'm a coward?
The sound of raucous singing in the distance.

ANDRI They're still singing.
The raucous singing dies away.

BARBLIN I never go out of the house now, so that they shall leave
me in peace. I think of you, Andri, all day long, when
you're at work, and now you're here and we're alone –
I want you to think of me, Andri, not of the others. Do
you hear? Only of me and of us. And I want you to be

proud, Andri, gay and proud, because I love you above all the others.

ANDRI I'm frightened when I feel proud.

BARBLIN And now I want you to kiss me.

Andri gives her a kiss.

No, kiss me properly!

Andri thinks.

I don't think of the others, Andri, when you hold me in your arms and kiss me, believe me, I don't think of them.

ANDRI But I do.

BARBLIN You and your 'others' all the time!

ANDRI I was tripped up again.

A tower-clock strikes.

I don't know in what way I'm different from everyone else. Tell me. In what way? I can't see it . . .

Another tower-clock strikes.

It's three o'clock already.

BARBLIN Let's go to sleep!

ANDRI I'm boring you.

Barblin says nothing.

Shall I put out the candle? . . . You can sleep, I'll wake you at seven.

Pause.

It isn't a superstition, oh no, there are people like that, people with a curse on them. I'm like that. It doesn't matter what I do, the others only have to look at me and suddenly I'm what they say I am. That's what evil is. Everyone has it in him, nobody wants it, so where is it to go to? Into the air? It is in the air, but it doesn't stay there long, it has to enter into a human being, so that one day they can seize it and kill it . . .

Andri takes hold of the candle.

Do you know a soldier named Peider?

Barblin mumbles sleepily

He's got his eye on you.

BARBLIN Him!

ANDRI I thought you were already asleep.

Andri blows out the candle.

FORESTAGE

The Carpenter enters the witness-box.

CARPENTER I admit that I asked fifty pounds for his apprenticeship because I didn't want his sort in my workshop, and I knew there would be trouble. Why didn't he want to be a salesman? I thought that would come naturally to him. Nobody could have known that he wasn't one. You know what I mean. I can only say that fundamentally I meant well by him. It's not my fault that things turned out as they did.

3

The sound of a lathe; a carpenter's shop. Andri and a journeyman carpenter, each with a finished chair.

ANDRI I've played outside left too, when there wasn't anyone else. I'd love to play, if your team will have me.
JOURNEYMAN Have you any football boots?
ANDRI No.
JOURNEYMAN Well, you can't play without them.
ANDRI How much do they cost?
JOURNEYMAN I've got an old pair, I'll sell them to you. Of course, you'll also need black shorts, and a yellow jersey, and yellow socks.
ANDRI I'm better on the right, but I can play on the left. I'm not bad at corners.
Andri rubs his hands.
That'll be smashing, Fedri, if it comes off.
JOURNEYMAN Why shouldn't it come off?
ANDRI That's smashing.
JOURNEYMAN I'm the captain and you're my friend.
ANDRI I'll go into training.

JOURNEYMAN But don't keep rubbing your hands together, otherwise
you'll have the crowd laughing at you.
Andri puts his hands in his trouser pockets.
Have you got a fag? Then give us one. He won't bawl
me out! If he did he'd be scared of his own voice. Have
you ever heard him bawl me out?
The Journeyman lights a cigarette.

ANDRI I'm glad you're my friend, Fedri.

JOURNEYMAN This your first chair?

ANDRI What do you think of it?
*The Journeyman takes Andri's chair and tries to pull the
leg off. Andri laughs.*
You won't pull those out.

JOURNEYMAN That's what he does.

ANDRI Go on, try!

CARPENTER [*off*] They said what?
The Journeyman tries in vain.

ANDRI He's coming.

JOURNEYMAN You're lucky.

ANDRI What do you mean lucky? Every proper chair is mortised.
Only those that are just stuck together fall apart.
Enter the Carpenter.

CARPENTER ... Write to them – tell them my name is Prader. A
chair by Prader doesn't collapse, every child knows that.
A chair by Prader is a chair by Prader. And anyhow,
paid is paid. In a word: I don't haggle.
To the two:
Are you on holiday?
The Journeyman dodges away fast.
Who has been smoking in here?
Andri doesn't answer.
I can smell it.
Andri says nothing.
Andri, if only you had the guts –

ANDRI Today is Saturday.

CARPENTER What has that to do with it?

ANDRI My apprenticeship test. You said, on the last Saturday
of the month. Here's my first chair.

The Carpenter takes the chair.

Not that one, Mr Prader, the other one.

CARPENTER It isn't easy to become a carpenter, it isn't easy at all if you don't have it in your blood. And how could it be in your blood? I told your father before you started. Why don't you go into selling? It's not easy if you haven't grown up with timber, you see, with our timber – you people may praise your cedars of Lebanon, but in this country we work in Andorran oak, my lad.

ANDRI That's beech.

CARPENTER Are you trying to teach me my job?

ANDRI I thought you were testing me.

CARPENTER *tries to pull out a leg of the chair.*

ANDRI Mr Prader, that isn't mine!

CARPENTER There –

The Carpenter pulls out the first leg.

What did I say?

The Carpenter pulls out the other three legs.

– Like frog's legs, like frog's legs. And I'm supposed to sell rubbish like that? A chair by Prader, do you know what that means? – There –

The Carpenter throws the debris down at his feet.

– just look at it!

ANDRI You're making a mistake.

CARPENTER Now, there's a chair!

The Carpenter sits on the other chair.

Fifteen stone I weigh, more's the pity, fifteen stone, but a proper chair doesn't groan when a real man sits on it, and it doesn't wobble. Does this chair groan?

ANDRI No.

CARPENTER Does it wobble?

ANDRI No.

CARPENTER There you are!

ANDRI That's my chair.

CARPENTER Then who made this rubbish?

ANDRI I told you at the beginning.

CARPENTER Fedri! Fedri!

The lathe stops.

I have nothing but trouble with you, that's the thanks
I get for taking your kind into the shop. I knew what it
would be like.
Enter the Journeyman.
Now, Fedri, are you a journeyman or what are you?

JOURNEYMAN I –

CARPENTER How long have you been with Prader & Son?

JOURNEYMAN Five years.

CARPENTER Which chair did you make?
This one or that rubbish over there? Answer.
The Journeyman looks at the débris.
Answer me frankly, which chair?

JOURNEYMAN I . . .

CARPENTER Did you mortise or didn't you?

JOURNEYMAN Every proper chair is mortised . . .

CARPENTER Do you hear that?

JOURNEYMAN Only those that are just stuck together fall apart . . .

CARPENTER You can go.

JOURNEYMAN *starts in alarm.*

CARPENTER Into the workshop, I mean.
The Journeyman hurries out.
Let that be a lesson to you. I knew your place wasn't in
a workshop.
The Carpenter sits down and fills his pipe.
A pity about the wasted timber.

ANDRI *says nothing.*

CARPENTER Have to use that for firewood.

ANDRI No.

CARPENTER *lights his pipe.*

ANDRI That's a dirty trick.

CARPENTER *lights his pipe.*

ANDRI I won't take back what I said. You're sitting on my chair,
I tell you, you lie whenever it suits you and light your
pipe. You, yes, you! I'm afraid of you, yes, I'm trembling.
Why have I no rights in your eyes? I'm young, I thought
to myself: I must be humble. There's no sense in it, you
take no notice of proof. You're sitting on my chair. You
don't give a damn about that. It makes no difference

what I do, you always twist it against me, and there's no end to your scorn. I can't keep silent any longer, it's burning me up. You're not even listening to me. You sit there sucking at your pipe and I tell you to your face: You're lying. You know perfectly well what a dirty trick you're playing. A rotten low-down trick. You're sitting on the chair I made and lighting your pipe. What harm have I done you? You don't want to admit that I'm any good. Why do you insult me? You all insult and jeer at me the whole time. How can you be stronger than the truth? You know very well what the truth is, you're sitting on it.

The Carpenter has at last lit his pipe.

You have no shame.

CARPENTER It's no good trying to get round me, lad.

ANDRI You look like a toad!

CARPENTER In the first place this isn't a Wailing Wall.

The Journeyman and two others give away their presence by giggling.

Do you want me to get rid of the lot of you?

The Journeyman and the two others disappear.

In the first place this isn't a Wailing Wall, in the second place I never said I was going to dismiss you. I didn't say that at all. I've got another job for you. Take off your apron! I'll show you how to write out orders. Are you listening when your master is speaking? For every order you bring in I'll give you ten shillings. Let's say a pound for three orders! That's what your kind have in their blood, believe me, and everyone should do what he has in his blood ... There's lots of money to be made, Andri, lots of money ...

Andri stands motionless.

Agreed?

The Carpenter stands up and slaps Andri on the back.

I've got your interests at heart.

The Carpenter goes. The lathe starts up again.

ANDRI But I wanted to be a carpenter ...

FORESTAGE

The Journeyman Carpenter, now in a motor-cyclist's jacket, enters the witness box.

JOURNEYMAN I admit that it was my chair and not his. At the time. I wanted to explain to him afterwards, but by then he was in such a state that it was impossible to talk to him. Afterwards I couldn't stand him either, I admit. He didn't even say good morning to us any more. I don't say he deserved it, but it was partly his fault, otherwise it would never have happened. When we asked him again about joining the team, he thought himself too good for us. It wasn't my fault that later they came and took him away.

4

A room in the Teacher's house. Andri is sitting being examined by a doctor, who is holding his tongue down with a spoon. Beside him the Mother.

ANDRI Aaaandorra.
DOCTOR But louder, my friend, much louder!
ANDRI Aaaaaaandorra.
DOCTOR Have you a longer spoon?
The Mother goes out.
How old are you?
ANDRI Twenty.
DOCTOR *lights a small cigar.*
ANDRI I've never been ill before.
DOCTOR You're a strong lad, I can see that, a good lad, a healthy lad, I like that, mens sana in corpore sano, if you know what that means.
ANDRI No.
DOCTOR What's your trade?
ANDRI I wanted to be a carpenter –

DOCTOR Let's have a look at your eyes!
The Doctor takes a magnifying glass out of his waistcoat pocket and examines Andri's eyes.
Now the other one!

ANDRI What's that thing you were talking about – a virus?

DOCTOR I used to know your father twenty years ago. I didn't know he had a son. The bull, we used to call him. Always charging straight at the wall. He got himself talked about in those days, a young teacher who tore up the school books; he wanted different ones and when he didn't get different ones he taught the Andorran children to under-line page by page in beautiful red pencil everything in the Andorran school books that isn't true. And they couldn't contradict him. What a fellow he was! Nobody knew what he was really after. A hell of a fellow. The ladies were very keen on him – oh, thank you very much –
Enter the Mother with a longer spoon.
I like your son!
The examination continues.
Carpentry is a fine trade, an Andorran trade; there are no carpenters anywhere in the world as good as the An-dorrans, that's well known.

ANDRI Aaaaaaaaaandorra!

DOCTOR Again.

ANDRI Aaaaaaaaaandorra!

MOTHER Is it serious, Doctor?

DOCTOR What do you mean, Doctor! My name is Ferrer.
The Doctor takes Andri's pulse.
Professor, to be exact, not that I attach any importance to titles, dear lady. The Andorran is sober and simple, they say, and there's some truth in it. The Andorran doesn't bow and scrape. I could have had titles by the dozen. Andorra is a republic. Take an example from her! With us everyone is valued for himself. I've said that all over the world. Why do you think I came back here again after twenty years?
The Doctor stops talking in order to count Andri's pulse.
H'm.

MOTHER   Is it serious, Professor?

DOCTOR   Dear lady, when a man has been around the world as I
have he knows the meaning of the word home. This is
my place, title or no title, this is where my roots are.
Andri coughs.
How long has he been coughing?

ANDRI   Since you lit your cigar.

DOCTOR   Andorra is a small country, but a free country. Where
else will you find that nowadays? No fatherland in the
world has a more beautiful name, and no people in the
world is so free. – Open your mouth, my friend, open
your mouth! Let's have another look at that throat.
*The Doctor looks into Andri's throat again, then he takes
out the spoon.*
A bit inflamed.

ANDRI   Me?

DOCTOR   Headache?

ANDRI   No.

DOCTOR   Insomnia?

ANDRI   Sometimes.

DOCTOR   Aha.

ANDRI   But not because of that.
The Doctor pushes the spoon down his throat again.

DOCTOR   Tongue down.

ANDRI   Aaaaaaaa-Aaaaaaaaaaaaaaaaaandorra.

DOCTOR   That's right, my friend, that's how it must ring out, so
that every Jew sinks into the ground when he hears the
name of our fatherland.
Andri winces.
Don't swallow the spoon!

MOTHER   Andri . . .

ANDRI   *has stood up.*

DOCTOR   Well, there's nothing much to worry about, a slight in-
flammation, he'll soon get over it, a pill before every
meal –

ANDRI   Why – should every Jew – sink into the ground?

DOCTOR   Where did I put them?
The Doctor rummages in his little bag.

You ask that, my young friend, because you haven't been out into the world. I know Jews. Wherever you go you find them already there, knowing everything better, and you, simple Andorran that you are, can pack up and go. That's the way it is. The worst thing about Jews is their ambition. In every country in the world they occupy all the university chairs, I know that from experience, and there's nothing left for us but our homeland. Mark you, I've nothing against Jews. I'm not in favour of atrocities. I saved the lives of Jews, although I can't stand the sight of them. And what thanks did I get? You can't change them. They occupy all the university chairs in the world. You can't change them.

The Doctor holds out the pills.

Here are your pills.

Andri doesn't take them but goes.

What's the matter with him all of a sudden?

MOTHER Andri! Andri!

DOCTOR Simply turning on his heel and going . . .

MOTHER You shouldn't have said that about Jews, Professor.

DOCTOR Why not?

MOTHER Andri is a Jew.

DOCTOR What!

Enter the Teacher, carrying exercise books.

TEACHER What's the matter?

MOTHER Nothing, don't excite yourself, nothing at all.

DOCTOR I wasn't to know that –

TEACHER Know what?

DOCTOR How is it that your son is a Jew?

TEACHER *says nothing.*

DOCTOR I must say, simply turning on his heel and going. I gave him medical treatment, even chatted with him, I explained to him what a virus is –

TEACHER I have work to do.

Silence.

MOTHER Andri is our foster-son.

TEACHER Goodbye.

DOCTOR Goodbye.

The Doctor takes his hat and bag.
I'm going.
The Doctor goes.

TEACHER What happened this time?

MOTHER Don't excite yourself!

TEACHER How did he get in here?

MOTHER He's the new medical officer.
Enter the Doctor again.

DOCTOR Let him take the pills just the same.
The Doctor takes off his hat.
I'm sorry about what happened.
The Doctor puts on his hat again.
What did I say . . . just because I said . . . I was joking,
of course, they can't take a joke, I can see that. Did anyone ever meet a Jew who could take a joke? Anyway I
never did . . . all I said was: I know Jews. I suppose one
is still allowed to speak the truth in Andorra . . .

TEACHER *says nothing.*

DOCTOR Where did I put my hat?

TEACHER *goes up to the Doctor, takes his hat from his head, opens the
door and throws out the hat.*
There's your hat.
The Doctor goes.

MOTHER I told you not to excite yourself. He'll never forgive you
for that. You quarrel with everybody and that doesn't
make things easier for Andri.

TEACHER Tell him to come here.

MOTHER Andri! Andri!

TEACHER That's the last straw. That man the medical officer. I
don't know what it is, but everything nowadays seems to
take the worst possible turn . . .
Enter Barblin and Andri.
Andri, you're not to take any notice of them. I'm not
going to put up with any injustice, you know that, Andri.

ANDRI Yes, Father.

TEACHER If that new medical officer of ours opens his stupid
mouth again, that pedant, that useless failure, that smug-
gler's son – I used to smuggle too, like every Andorran,

but I don't stick titles in front of my name – if he opens
his stupid mouth again he'll be thrown down the steps
himself and not just his hat.
To the Mother:
I'm not afraid of them!
To Andri:
And you're not to be afraid of them either, understand?
If we stick together, you and me, like men, Andri, like
friends, like father and son – or haven't I treated you like
a son? Have I ever neglected you? If I have, say to my
face. Have I treated you differently from my daughter?
Tell me so to my face. I'm waiting.

ANDRI What do you want me to say, Father?

TEACHER I can't bear it when you stand there like a choir boy who
has been caught stealing or something, so well behaved –
is it because you're afraid of me? I know I fly off the
handle sometimes, I suppose I'm unjust. I haven't made
a note of all my mistakes as an educator.

MOTHER *lays the table.*

TEACHER Has your Mother ever treated you heartlessly?

MOTHER What are you making a speech for? Anyone would think
you were addressing a meeting.

TEACHER I'm speaking to Andri.

MOTHER I see.

TEACHER Man to man.

MOTHER Supper's ready.
The Mother goes out.

TEACHER That's really all I wanted to say to you.

BARBLIN *finishes laying the table.*

TEACHER If he's such a big noise abroad, why doesn't he stay there,
this professor who didn't even manage to get his doc-
torate at any university in the world? This patriot who's
now our medical officer because he can't construct a
single sentence without using the words homeland and
Andorra? Whose fault is it if his ambition came to
nothing, whose fault could it be if not the Jews? – Jew!
I'm sick of the word. I never want to hear it again.

MOTHER *brings the soup.*

TEACHER And you're not to use that word either, Andri. Understand? I won't tolerate it. You don't know what you're
saying, and I don't want you to end up by believing what
they say. Just remember, there's nothing in it. Once and
for all. Understand? Once and for all.

MOTHER Have you finished?

TEACHER There's nothing in it.

MOTHER Then cut the bread for us.

TEACHER *cuts the bread.*

ANDRI I wanted to ask you something else . . .

MOTHER *ladles out the soup.*

ANDRI Perhaps you know already. Nothing has happened,
there's no need for you to worry. I don't know the right
way to say a thing like this. – I'm almost twenty-one
and Barblin is nineteen . . .

TEACHER What of it?

ANDRI We want to get married.

TEACHER *drops the bread.*

ANDRI Yes. I've come to ask – I meant to do it when I had
passed my carpentry test, but you know what happened
about that. – We want to become engaged now, so that
the others know and don't keep running after Barblin
wherever she goes.

TEACHER Married!

ANDRI I am asking you, Father, for the hand of your daughter.

TEACHER *rises like a prisoner upon whom sentence has been passed.*

MOTHER I've seen it coming, Can.

TEACHER Quiet!

MOTHER It's no reason to get so upset.
The Mother picks up the bread from the floor.
They love each other.

TEACHER Be quiet!
Silence.

ANDRI But that's the way it is, Father, we love each other. It's
hard to talk about it. Ever since we shared the green bed-
room as children we have talked about getting married.
At school we felt embarrassed because everyone laughed
at us. You can't do that, they said, because you're brother

and sister! Once we made up our minds to poison ourselves, because we were brother and sister, with deadly
nightshade, but it was winter and there wasn't any deadly
nightshade. And we cried, until Mother noticed – till you
came, Mother, and comforted us and told us we were not
brother and sister. And the whole story, how father
smuggled me across the frontier, because I'm a Jew. And
I was very happy about it and told them at school and
everywhere. Since then we haven't slept in the same
room; we're not children any more.

The Teacher remains silent as though turned to stone.

It is time we were married, Father.

TEACHER Andri, that's impossible.

MOTHER Why?

TEACHER Because it's impossible!

MOTHER Don't shout.

TEACHER No – No – No . . .

BARBLIN *bursts into tears.*

MOTHER And don't you start howling straight away!

BARBLIN I shall kill myself.

MOTHER And don't talk rubbish!

BARBLIN Or I shall go to the soldiers, I shall.

MOTHER Then may God punish you!

BARBLIN Let him.

ANDRI Barblin?

BARBLIN *runs out.*

TEACHER Let her go. She's a silly goose. There are lots of other
girls.

Andri tears himself away from him.

Andri – !

ANDRI She may do something crazy.

TEACHER Stay here.

Andri stays.

I've never had to say no to you before, Andri.

The Teacher holds both hands over his face.

No!

MOTHER I don't understand you, Can, I don't understand you.
Are you jealous? Barblin is nineteen and someone is

going to come along. Why not Andri, whom we know? That's the way of the world. Why do you stare into space and shake your head? I think we're very lucky. Why won't you give your daughter to Andri? You say nothing. Do you want to marry her yourself? You keep silent because you're jealous, Can, jealous of the youngsters and of life in general, because now it is going on without you.

TEACHER What do you know about it!

MOTHER I'm only asking.

TEACHER Barblin is still a child –

MOTHER That's what all fathers say. A child! – To you, Can, but not to Andri.

TEACHER *says nothing.*

MOTHER Why do you say No?

TEACHER *says nothing.*

ANDRI Because I'm a Jew.

TEACHER Andri –

ANDRI Go on, say it.

TEACHER Jew! Jew!

ANDRI That's it.

TEACHER Jew! Every third word I hear is Jew, every second word, there's not a day without Jew, not a night without Jew, I hear Jew when someone snores, Jew, Jew, not a joke without Jew, not a business deal without Jew, not a curse without Jew, I hear Jew where there is no Jew, Jew and Jew and again Jew, in school the children play Jew when I turn my back, everyone babbles it after everyone else, the horses neigh it in the streets: Jeeeew, Jeew, Jew . . .

MOTHER You're exaggerating.

TEACHER Aren't there any other reasons any more?

MOTHER Then tell us them.

TEACHER *says nothing, then takes his hat.*

MOTHER Where are you going?

TEACHER Where I can find peace and quiet.
He goes, slamming the door behind him.

MOTHER Now he'll drink till midnight again.
Andri walks slowly across to the other side.
Andri? – Now they're all parted.

5

*The square of Andorra. The Teacher is sitting alone outside
the inn. The Innkeeper brings the brandy which he has
ordered but which he does not at first pick up.*

INNKEEPER What's new?

TEACHER Another brandy.

The Innkeeper goes.

Because I'm a Jew!

He now drains the brandy.

Some day I shall tell them the truth – at least that's what
one says; but a lie is a leech, it sucks the truth dry. It
grows. I shall never shake it off. It grows and is full of
blood. It looks at me like a son, flesh and blood, a Jew,
my son . . . What's new? – I lied and you fondled him,
so long as he was still a child, but now he is a man, now
he wants to marry, wants to marry his sister. – That's
something new! . . . I know already what you will think:
Even a Jew-rescuer thinks his own child too good for a
Jew! I can already see your grins.

Enter the Somebody, who sits down with the Teacher.

SOMEBODY What's new?

TEACHER *says nothing.*

SOMEBODY *opens his newspaper.*

TEACHER What are you grinning at?

SOMEBODY They're threatening again.

TEACHER Who?

SOMEBODY The people across the border.

The Teacher rises; the Innkeeper comes out.

INNKEEPER Where are you off to?

TEACHER Where I can find peace and quiet.

The Teacher goes into the inn.

SOMEBODY What's got into him? If he carries on like that, he'll come
to a sticky end, if you ask me . . . I'll have a beer.

The Innkeeper goes.

At least you can get some peace here now that lad's gone. He was always wasting his tips on that juke box.

6

Outside Barblin's room. Andri is sleeping on the threshold. Candlelight. A large shadow appears on the wall: the Soldier. Andri snores. The Soldier takes fright and hesitates. A tower-clock strikes the hour. The Soldier sees that Andri does not stir and ventures to the door, hesitates again, opens the door. Another clock strikes the hour. The Soldier now steps over the sleeping Andri and, having got so far, enters the darkened room. Barblin tries to scream, but the Soldier puts his hand over her mouth. Silence. Andri wakes.

ANDRI Barblin? . . .

Now it's quiet again outside, they've finished boozing and bawling, they've all gone home to bed.
Silence.
Are you asleep, Barblin? What time is it? I've been asleep. Four o'clock? The night is like milk, Barblin, like blue milk. Soon the birds will start. Like a Flood of milk . . .
A sound.
Why are you bolting the door?
Silence.
Let your father come up, let him find me on his daughter's threshold. I don't care! I shan't give up, Barblin, I shall sit here every night, even if he drinks himself to death over there, every night.
He takes a cigarette.
I'm wide awake again now.
He sits and smokes.
I don't slink about like a begging dog any more. I hate. I don't shed any tears now. I laugh. The meaner they

behave towards me, the more comfortable I feel in my hate. And the more confident. Hate makes plans. I feel good every day now because I have a plan and no one knows about it, and if I walk about timidly I'm only pretending. Hate makes you cunning. Hate makes you proud. One day I'll show them. Since I have hated them there are times when I feel like whistling and singing, but I don't do it. Hate makes you patient. Hate makes you hard. I hate their country that we are going to leave, and I hate their faces. I love one single person, and that is enough.

He listens.

The cat's awake too!

He counts coins.

I made thirty shillings today, Barblin, thirty shillings in a single day. I'm saving now. I don't go to the juke-box any more.

He laughs.

If they could see how right they are: I'm always counting my money!

He listens.

There goes another one shuffling off home.

The twittering of birds.

I saw that Peider yesterday, you know, the one who fancies you, the one who tripped me up; he grins every time he sees me now, but I don't care –

He listens.

He's coming up!

Footsteps in the house.

We've got forty-one pounds now, Barblin, but don't tell anyone. We'll get married. Believe me, there's another world where nobody knows us, where nobody will trip me up; that's where we'll go, Barblin. He can yell himself hoarse here if he wants to.

He smokes.

I'm glad you have bolted the door.

Enter the Teacher.

TEACHER My son!

ANDRI I'm not your son.

TEACHER Andri, I've come to tell you the truth, before the night's over . . .

ANDRI You've been drinking.

TEACHER Only on your account, Andri, only on your account.
Andri laughs.
My son –

ANDRI Stop that!

TEACHER Are you listening to me?

ANDRI Hang onto a lamp-post, not me, I can smell you.
Andri frees himself.
And don't keep saying 'My son!' all the time. It's only because you're tight.

TEACHER *staggers.*

ANDRI Your daughter has bolted her door, don't worry.

TEACHER Andri –

ANDRI You can't stand up.

TEACHER I'm worried.

ANDRI There's no need.

TEACHER Very worried . . .

ANDRI Look, Mother is crying, she's waiting up for you.

TEACHER I didn't reckon with that . . .

ANDRI What didn't you reckon with?

TEACHER That you would refuse to be my son.
Andri laughs.
I must sit down . . .

ANDRI Then I'm going.

TEACHER So you won't listen?

ANDRI *takes the candle.*

TEACHER All right, then don't.

ANDRI I owe you my life. I know. If you attach importance to it I can repeat it once a day: I owe you my life. Twice a day if you like: I owe you my life. Once in the morning, once in the evening: I owe you my life, I owe you my life.

TEACHER Andri, I've been drinking, all night long, so that I could come and tell you the truth – I know I've had too much . . .

ANDRI That's what I think too.

TEACHER Andri, you do owe me your life.

ANDRI Thank you for it.

TEACHER You don't understand what I mean . . .

ANDRI *says nothing.*

TEACHER Don't just stand there like that! – I wanted to tell you about my life . . .
Cocks crow.
But you're not interested in my life.

ANDRI I'm interested in my own life.
Cocks crow.
It's morning already.

TEACHER *staggers.*

ANDRI Don't pretend you can still think.

TEACHER You despise me, don't you?

ANDRI I'm just looking at you. That's all. I used to respect you. Not because you saved my life, but because I thought you weren't like all the others; you didn't think their thoughts, you had courage. I relied on you. And then I found out the truth, and now I'm looking at you.

TEACHER What is the truth?

ANDRI *says nothing.*

TEACHER I don't think their thoughts, Andri. I tore up their school books. I wanted them to have others –

ANDRI Everyone knows that.

TEACHER Do you know what I did?

ANDRI I'm going.

TEACHER I asked you if you knew what I did . . .

ANDRI You tore up their school books.

TEACHER I lied.
Pause.
You refuse to understand me . . .
Cocks crow.

ANDRI At seven I have to be in the shop, selling chairs, selling tables, selling cupboards, rubbing my hands.

TEACHER Why do you have to rub your hands?

ANDRI 'Could you find a better chair? Does it wobble? Does it creak? Could you find a cheaper chair?'

The Teacher stares at him.

I have to make money.

TEACHER Why do you have to make money?

ANDRI Because I'm a Jew.

TEACHER My son – !

ANDRI Stop that!

TEACHER *staggers.*

ANDRI You're disgusting.

TEACHER Andri –

ANDRI Stop snivelling.

TEACHER Andri –

ANDRI Push off.

TEACHER What did you say?

ANDRI It's coming out of your eyes; if you can't hold your drink, then go to bed.

TEACHER Do you hate me?

ANDRI *says nothing.*

The Teacher goes.

He has gone, Barblin, I didn't want to hurt his feelings. But things get worse and worse. Did you hear him? He doesn't know what he's saying any more, and then you'd think he really was crying – Barblin – are you asleep?

He listens at the door.

Barblin! Barblin!

He shakes the door, then tries to break it open. He starts to run at it again, but at this moment the door is opened from inside: in the doorway stands the Soldier, lit by the candle, barefoot, the belt of his trousers undone, naked to the waist.

Barblin . . .

SOLDIER Beat it.

ANDRI That can't be true . . .

SOLDIER Beat it, or I'll smash your face in.

FORESTAGE

The Soldier, now in civilian clothes, enters the witness box.

SOLDIER I admit I never liked him. I didn't know that he wasn't one, everybody said he was one. As a matter of fact I still think he was one. I didn't like him from the start. But I didn't kill him. I only did my duty. Orders are orders. What would the world come to if orders weren't carried out? I was a soldier.

7

Sacristy, the Priest and Andri

PRIEST Andri, we must have a talk together. Your foster-mother is very worried about you . . . Sit down!

ANDRI *says nothing.*

PRIEST Do sit down, Andri!

ANDRI *says nothing.*

PRIEST You won't sit down?

ANDRI *says nothing.*

PRIEST I can understand, this is the first time you've been here. More or less. I remember they once sent you to fetch your football from behind the altar when it came sailing in.

The Priest laughs.

ANDRI What do you want to talk about, Father?

PRIEST Sit down!

ANDRI *says nothing.*

PRIEST You don't want to sit down?

ANDRI *says nothing.*

PRIEST Very well then.

ANDRI Is it true, Father, that I am different from everyone else?

Pause.

PRIEST Andri, I want to tell you something.

ANDRI I'm insolent, I know.

PRIEST I understand your distress. But you must know that we like you, Andri, just as you are. Hasn't your foster-father done everything he could for you? I hear he sold land so that you could become a carpenter.

ANDRI But I'm not going to become a carpenter.

PRIEST Why not?

ANDRI My sort think of nothing but money all the time, people say, so my place isn't in the workshop, says the carpenter, but in the salesroom. I'm going to be a salesman, Father.

PRIEST Very well then.

ANDRI But I wanted to be a carpenter.

PRIEST Why don't you sit down?

ANDRI I think you're mistaken, Father, people don't like me. The innkeeper says I'm insolent, and the carpenter thinks so too, I believe. And the doctor says I'm ambitious, and my sort have no backbone.

PRIEST Sit down!

ANDRI Do you think I've no backbone, Father?

PRIEST It may be that there is something restless about you, Andri.

ANDRI And Peider says I'm a coward.

PRIEST A coward? Why?

ANDRI Because I'm a Jew.

PRIEST Fancy paying attention to Peider!

ANDRI *says nothing.*

PRIEST Andri, I want to tell you something.

ANDRI I know – I shouldn't keep thinking of myself all the time. But I can't help it, Father. I can't help wondering all the time whether what people say about me is true: that I'm not like them, not gay, not jolly, just not like them. And you too think there is something restless about me, Father, you've just said so. I can quite understand that nobody likes me. I don't like myself when I think about myself.

The Priest stands up.

Can I go now?

PRIEST Now listen to me!

ANDRI What do people want from me, Father?

PRIEST Why are you so suspicious?

ANDRI They all put their hands on my shoulder.

PRIEST Do you know what you are, Andri?

The Priest laughs.

You don't know, so I shall tell you.

Andri stares at him.

A splendid fellow! In your own way. A splendid fellow!
I have been watching you, Andri, for years!

ANDRI Watching?

PRIEST Of course.

ANDRI Why does everyone watch me?

PRIEST I like you, Andri, more than all the others, yes, precisely
because you are different from all the others. Why do you
shake your head? You are cleverer than they are. Indeed
you are. I like that about you, Andri, and I'm glad that
you have come to see me and that I have had the chance
to tell you so.

ANDRI It's not true.

PRIEST What isn't true?

ANDRI I'm not different. I don't want to be different. And even
if he's three times stronger than me, that Peider, I'll beat
the daylight out of him in front of everybody in the
square; I've sworn that to myself –

PRIEST As far as I'm concerned you're welcome to.

ANDRI I've sworn to do it –

PRIEST I don't like him either.

ANDRI I don't want to be popular. I shall stand up for myself.
I'm not a coward – and I'm not cleverer than the others,
Father; I don't want you to say that.

PRIEST Will you listen to me now?

ANDRI No.

Andri draws away.

I don't like having everyone's hands on my shoulders
the whole time.

Pause.

PRIEST You really don't make it easy for one.

Pause.

To be brief, your foster-mother came to see me. She was here for more than four hours. The good woman is very unhappy. You don't come home to meals any more, she says, and you won't talk to anyone. She says you don't believe that people are thinking of your wellbeing.

ANDRI Everyone is thinking of my wellbeing!

PRIEST Why do you laugh?

ANDRI If he's thinking of my wellbeing, Father, why is he willing to give me everything, but not his own daughter, why?

PRIEST It is his right as a father –

ANDRI But why? Why? Because I'm a Jew.

PRIEST Don't shout!

ANDRI *says nothing.*

PRIEST Haven't you any other idea in your head? I have told you, Andri, as a Christian, that I love you – but you have one unfortunate habit, I'm afraid I must say, all of you: whatever difficulties you come up against in life, you attribute absolutely everything to the fact that you are Jews. You really don't make things easy for one with your over-sensitiveness.

ANDRI *says nothing.*

PRIEST You're crying.

ANDRI *sobs, covering his face with his hands.*

PRIEST What has happened? Answer me. What's the matter? I'm asking you what has happened. Andri! Why don't you speak, Andri? You're shivering. You've lost your senses. How can I help you if you don't speak? Pull yourself together, Andri! Do you hear? Andri! Remember you're a man! Well, I don't know.

ANDRI Barblin!
Andri lets his hands fall from his face and stares in front of him.
She can't love me, no one can, I can't love myself . . .
Enter a sacristan with a chasuble.
Can I go now?
The Sacristan unbuttons the Priest.

PRIEST You can stay.

The Sacristan dresses the Priest for Mass.

You've said it yourself: how can other people love us if we don't love ourselves? Our Lord said: Love thy neighbour as thyself. He said: As thyself. We must accept ourselves, and that is what you don't do, Andri. Why do you want to be like the others? You're cleverer than they, believe me, you're more alert. Why won't you admit that? There is a spark in you. Why do you play football like all those boneheads, and rush about the field shouting, simply in order to be an Andorran? They don't like you, I know. And I know why. There's a spark in you. You think. Why shouldn't there also be some among God's creatures who have more intelligence than feeling? I tell you, that is exactly what I admire about you people. Why do you look at me like that? There is a spark in all of you. Think of Einstein! And all the rest of them, whatever their names are. Think of Spinoza!

ANDRI Can I go now?

PRIEST No man can change his skin, Andri, no Jew and no Christian. Nobody. God wants us to be as he created us. Do you understand me? And when they say to you: Jews are cowards, then know that you are not a coward if you accept being a Jew. On the contrary. You are different from us. Do you hear me? I say: You are not a coward. Only if you try to be like all Andorrans, then you are a coward . . .

An organ starts to play.

ANDRI Can I go now?

PRIEST Think over what you yourself said, Andri: How can the others accept you, if you don't accept yourself?

ANDRI Can I go now . . .

PRIEST Andri, have you understood me?

FORESTAGE

The Priest kneels.

PRIEST Thou shalt not make unto thee any graven image of the
Lord, thy God, nor of men who are his creatures. I too
was guilty at that time. I wanted to meet him with love
when I spoke with him. I too made an image of him, I
too put fetters on him. I too bound him to the stake.

8

*The square of Andorra. The Doctor is the only one sitting;
the others are standing: the Innkeeper, the Soldier, the
Journeyman, the Somebody.*

SOLDIER I say it's disgusting
DOCTOR I say, keep calm!
SOLDIER Why can't Andorra be attacked?
DOCTOR *lights a small cigar.*
SOLDIER I say it's disgusting.
INNKEEPER Was I to say there isn't a decent room in Andorra? I'm
an innkeeper. You can't turn a foreigneress away from
your door –
SOMEBODY *laughs.*
INNKEEPER What else could I do? A Señora stands there and asks if
there's a decent room –
SOLDIER A Señora, listen to him!
CARPENTER A woman from over the border?
SOLDIER Any trouble and we'll fight to the last man – and he puts
her up!
He spits on the asphalt.
I say it's disgusting!
DOCTOR Don't get excited.
He smokes.
I've been around the world and I know. I'm an Andorran,
everyone knows that, an Andorran body and soul. Other-

wise I shouldn't have come back home, you good people;
otherwise your professor wouldn't have renounced all
the university chairs in the world –

SOMEBODY *laughs.*

INNKEEPER What is there to laugh about?

SOMEBODY Who is going to fight to the last man?

SOLDIER I am.

SOMEBODY In the Bible it says, the last shall be first, or the other
way round, I don't remember, the first shall be last.

SOLDIER What does he mean by that?

SOMEBODY I'm only asking.

SOLDIER To the last man, that's an order. Rather dead than a
slave, that's pasted on the wall in every barracks. That's
an order. Let them come, they'll get the shock of their
lives . . .
Brief silence.

CARPENTER Why can't Andorra be attacked?

DOCTOR I am aware that the situation is tense.

CARPENTER Tenser than it's ever been before.

DOCTOR It's been that for years.

CARPENTER Why have they massed troops on the frontier?

DOCTOR What I was going to say was this: I've been around in
the world. One thing you can take from me: there is no
people in the whole world so universally beloved as we
are. That's a fact.

CARPENTER True enough.

DOCTOR Bearing that fact in mind, let us ask ourselves, what
can happen to a country like Andorra? Quite object-
ively.

INNKEEPER That's right, that's right.

SOLDIER What's right?

INNKEEPER No country is so much loved as we are.

CARPENTER True enough.

DOCTOR Loved isn't the word for it. I have met people who had
no idea where Andorra was, but every child in the world
knows that Andorra is a sanctuary, a sanctuary of peace
and freedom and human rights.

INNKEEPER Very true.

DOCTOR Andorra is an idea, the incarnation of an idea, if you know what that means.

He smokes.

I say, they won't dare.

SOLDIER Why not, why not?

INNKEEPER Because we are the incarnation of an idea.

SOLDIER But they outnumber us!

INNKEEPER Because we are so loved.

The Idiot brings a lady's suitcase and puts it down.

SOLDIER Just look at that!

The Idiot leaves again.

CARPENTER What does she want here?

JOURNEYMAN A spyess!

SOLDIER What else?

JOURNEYMAN A spyess!

SOLDIER And he's putting her up!

SOMEBODY *laughs.*

SOLDIER What are you grinning at?

SOMEBODY Spyess is rich.

SOLDIER What else can she be?

SOMEBODY The word isn't spyess, but spy, even if the situation is tense and if the individual is female.

CARPENTER I wonder what she has come for really.

The Idiot brings a second lady's suitcase.

SOLDIER Just look at that!

JOURNEYMAN Let's kick her stuff to pieces!

INNKEEPER That would be the last straw.

The Idiot leaves again.

Instead of taking the luggage upstairs, the idiot runs off and leaves it, and it attracts everybody's attention –

SOMEBODY *laughs.*

INNKEEPER I'm not a traitor, am I, Professor? That's not true. I'm an innkeeper. I should be the first to throw a stone. Indeed I should! There's still a law of hospitality in Andorra, an ancient and sacred law. Isn't that so, Professor, isn't that so? An innkeeper can't say no, however tense the situation may be, and certainly not when it's a lady.

SOMEBODY *laughs.*

JOURNEYMAN And when she has dough!

SOMEBODY *laughs.*

INNKEEPER The situation is no laughing matter.

SOMEBODY Spyess.

INNKEEPER Leave her luggage alone!

SOMEBODY Spyess is very good.
The Idiot brings a lady's coat and puts it down.

SOLDIER Just look at that!
The Idiot leaves again.

CARPENTER Why do you think Andorra can't be attacked?

DOCTOR You aren't listening to me.
He smokes.
I thought you were listening to me.
He smokes.
They won't dare, I say. No matter how many tanks they have, and parachutes on top of that, they simply can't afford to. Or as Perin, our great poet, once said: Our weapon is our innocence. Or the other way round: Our innocence is our weapon. Where else in the world is there a republic which can say that? I ask you: Where? A people like us, who can appeal to the conscience of the world like no other, a people without guilt –
Andri appears in the background.

SOLDIER There he goes slinking around again!
Andri withdraws, because everyone is looking at him.

DOCTOR Andorrans, let me tell you something. No nation in the world has ever been attacked unless there was some offence it could be reproached with. What can they reproach us with? The only thing that could happen to Andorra would be an injustice, a crude and blatant injustice. And they won't dare to do that. They won't dare tomorrow any more than yesterday. Because the whole world would defend us. In a flash. Because the conscience of the whole world is on our side.

SOMEBODY In a flash.

INNKEEPER Will you keep your trap shut for a change!

SOMEBODY *laughs.*

DOCTOR Who are you, anyhow?

SOMEBODY A man with a sense of humour.

DOCTOR Your sense of humour is out of place.

JOURNEYMAN *kicks the cases.*

INNKEEPER Stop!

DOCTOR What's the idea?

INNKEEPER For heaven's sake!

SOMEBODY *laughs.*

DOCTOR What a stupid thing to do. That's just what they're waiting for. Interference with travellers in Andorra! So that they have an excuse to attack us. What a stupid thing to do! Just when I'm telling you to keep calm! We won't give them an excuse – spy or no spy.

INNKEEPER *puts the cases straight again.*

SOLDIER I say it's disgusting!

INNKEEPER *wipes the cases clean.*

DOCTOR It's a good job no one saw . . .

Enter the Señora. Silence. The Señora sits down at an empty table. The Andorrans eye her as she slowly takes off her gloves.

Here's what I owe you? I'm off.

CARPENTER So am I.

The Doctor rises and leaves, raising his hat to the lady as he goes; the Carpenter signs to the Journeyman to follow him too.

SEÑORA Has something been happening here?

SOMEBODY *laughs.*

SEÑORA Can I have something to drink?

INNKEEPER With pleasure, Señora –

SEÑORA What do people drink in this country?

INNKEEPER Anything you like, Señora –

SEÑORA I'd really prefer a glass of cold water.

INNKEEPER Señora, we have everything.

SOMEBODY *laughs.*

INNKEEPER The gentleman has a sense of humour.

SOMEBODY *goes.*

SEÑORA The room is very nice, innkeeper, very nice.

INNKEEPER *bows and leaves.*

SOLDIER And a whisky for me!

The Soldier stays and sits down in order to stare at the Señora. On the forestage right, by the juke-box, Andri appears and drops in a coin.

INNKEEPER You're always at that damned juke-box!

ANDRI I pay.

INNKEEPER Don't you ever think of anything else?

ANDRI No.

While the same record goes on playing: The Señora writes a note; the Soldier stares; she folds the note and speaks to the Soldier, without looking at him.

SEÑORA Aren't there any women in Andorra?

The Idiot comes back.

Do you know a teacher named Can?

The Idiot grins and nods.

Take him this note, please.

Enter three other soldiers and the Journeyman.

SOLDIER Did you hear that? Aren't there any women in Andorra, she asked me.

JOURNEYMAN What did you say?

SOLDIER No, but there are men!

JOURNEYMAN Did you say that?

SOLDIER I asked her if she came to Andorra because there aren't any men across the border.

JOURNEYMAN Did you say that?

SOLDIER That's what I said.

They grin.

Here he comes. As white as chalk! He wants to beat me up. Did you know that?

Enter Andri. The music has stopped.

How's your fiancée?

ANDRI *seizes the Soldier by the collar.*

SOLDIER What's the idea.

The Soldier frees himself.

Some old rabbi has been telling him about David and Goliath; now he wants to play David.

They grin.

Let's go.

ANDRI Fedri –

JOURNEYMAN How he stammers!

ANDRI Why did you betray me?

SOLDIER Let's go.
Andri knocks the Soldier's cap off his head.
Now you watch it!
The Soldier picks the cap up from the ground and dusts it.
If you think I'm going to get put in the glasshouse
because of you –

JOURNEYMAN What the hell does he want?

ANDRI Now smash my face in.

SOLDIER Let's go.
*The Soldier puts on his cap, Andri knocks it off again, the
others laugh, the Soldier suddenly gives him an uppercut
and Andri goes down.*
Where's your sling, David?
Andri gets up.
Now watch our David cut loose!
*Andri suddenly gives the Soldier an uppercut, and the Sol-
dier goes down.*
You damn Jew – !

SEÑORA No! No! All against one. No!
*The other soldiers have seized hold of Andri, so that the
Soldier gets away. The Soldier lashes out at Andri while
the others are holding him. Andri defends himself silently,
then suddenly breaks loose. The Journeyman kicks him from
behind. When Andri turns round the Soldier attacks him
from behind. Andri falls. The four soldiers and the Journeyman kick him from all sides, until they notice the Señora,
who has come up to them.*

SOLDIER That's the last straw, making us look ridiculous in front
of a foreigner . . .
The Soldier and the others make off.

SEÑORA Who are you?

ANDRI I'm not a coward.

SEÑORA What's your name?

ANDRI They're always saying I'm a coward.

SEÑORA No, no, don't touch the wound!
Enter the Innkeeper with a carafe and glass on a tray.

INNKEEPER What's happened?

SEÑORA Get a doctor.

INNKEEPER And in front of my hotel – !

SEÑORA Give me that.

The Señora takes the carafe and her handkerchief and kneels down beside Andri, who tries to sit up.

They kicked him with their boots.

INNKEEPER Impossible, Señora!

SEÑORA Don't just stand there, fetch a doctor.

INNKEEPER Señora, this sort of thing isn't usual here . . .

SEÑORA I'm only cleaning it.

INNKEEPER It's your own fault. Why do you always come when the soldiers are here . . . ?

SEÑORA Look at me!

INNKEEPER I've warned you.

SEÑORA Luckily it's missed your eye.

INNKEEPER It's his own fault, Señora, he's always going to the juke-box, I've warned him. He gets on people's nerves . . .

SEÑORA Will you please fetch a doctor?

The Innkeeper goes.

ANDRI Now they're all against me.

SEÑORA Is it hurting you?

ANDRI I don't need a doctor.

SEÑORA It's gone right down to the bone.

ANDRI I know the doctor.

Andri stands up.

I can walk, it's only my forehead.

SEÑORA *stands up.*

ANDRI I'm sorry, I've spoilt your handkerchief.

SEÑORA Take me to your father.

The Señora takes Andri's arm and they walk slowly away while the Innkeeper and the Doctor come.

DOCTOR Arm in arm?

INNKEEPER They kicked him with their boots, I saw it with my own eyes, I was inside.

DOCTOR *lights a small cigar.*

INNKEEPER He's always going to the juke-box, I've told him about it. He gets on people's nerves.

DOCTOR Blood?

INNKEEPER I saw it coming.

DOCTOR *smokes.*

INNKEEPER Why don't you say anything?

DOCTOR A nasty business.

INNKEEPER He started it.

DOCTOR I have nothing against these people, but I feel uncomfortable the moment I set eyes on one of them. However you behave, it's wrong. What did I say? They can't leave well alone, they're always asking us to prove ourselves by our attitude to them. As though we had nothing else to do! No one likes to have a guilty conscience, but that's what they bank on. They want us to do them an injustice. That's all they're waiting for . . .

He turns to go.

Wash that little bit of blood away. And don't gossip! There's no need to tell people what you saw.

FORESTAGE

The Teacher and the Señora outside the white house as at the beginning.

SEÑORA You said our son was a Jew.

TEACHER *says nothing.*

SEÑORA Why did you put that lie into the world?

TEACHER *says nothing.*

SEÑORA One day an Andorran peddlar came by. He was very talkative. To praise Andorra he told everyone the touching story of a teacher from here, who had saved a Jewish child at the time of the great murder and now cares for him as if he were his own son. I immediately sent a letter: Are you this teacher? I wrote. I demanded an answer. Why do you say he is a Jewish child? I asked: Do you know what you have done? I waited for an answer. It didn't come. Perhaps you never got my letter. I couldn't believe what I feared. I wrote a second letter,

and a third. I waited for an answer. So time passed . . .
Why did you put that lie into the world?

TEACHER Why, why, why!

SEÑORA You hated me when the child was born because I was a
coward, because I was afraid of my people. When you
came to the frontier, you said it was a Jewish child whom
you had saved from us. Why? Because you too were a
coward when you returned home. Because you too were
afraid of your people.

Pause.

Wasn't it like that?

Pause.

Perhaps you wanted to show that you Andorrans are
quite different from us. Because you hated me. But the
people here are not different, you can see that, not very
different.

TEACHER *says nothing.*

SEÑORA He must know the truth. Which of us is going to tell
him?

TEACHER I will, I'll tell him.

SEÑORA And will you tell them?

TEACHER Yes, I'll tell them that he is my son, our son, their own
flesh and blood.

SEÑORA Why don't you go and tell them?

TEACHER Suppose they don't want the truth?

Interval

9

A room in the Teacher's house. The Señora is seated, Andri standing.

SEÑORA *puts on one glove.*
Noise in the street.

SEÑORA I'm glad to have seen you.

ANDRI Are you leaving us, Señora?

SEÑORA I have been asked to go.

ANDRI If you say no country is worse and no country is better than Andorra, why don't you stay here?

SEÑORA Would you like me to? Do you know that you are handsome?
Noise in the street.
They have treated you badly, Andri, but that will stop now. The truth will put them right; and you are the only one here who need not fear the truth.

ANDRI What truth?
Noise in the street.

SEÑORA I must go. I'm from the other side of the frontier, you can hear how I exasperate them. A Black! That's what they call us here, I know . . .
She puts on the other glove.
There are lots of other things I should like to tell you, and a lot of things I should like to ask. I should like to have a long talk with you. But we shall see each other again, I hope . . .
She is ready.
We shall see each other again.
She looks round once more.
So this is where you grew up?

ANDRI Yes.
Noise in the street.

SEÑORA I ought to go now.
She remains seated.
When I was your age – that time goes very quickly, Andri, you're twenty now and can't believe it: people meet,

love, part, life is in front of you, and when you look in
the mirror, all of a sudden it is behind you. You don't
seem to yourself very different, but suddenly it is other
people who are twenty . . . When I was your age – my
father, who was in the army, had been killed in the war.
I knew how he thought, and I didn't want to think like
him. We wanted a different world. We were young like
you, and what we were taught was murderous, we knew
that. And we despised the world as it is, we saw through
it and dared to want another one. And we tried to create
another one. We wanted not to be afraid of people. Not
for anything in the world. We didn't want to lie. When
we saw that we were merely keeping silent about our fear,
we hated each other. Our new world didn't last long. We
crossed the frontiers again, back to where we had come
from when we were as young as you . . .
She rises.
Do you understand what I'm saying?

ANDRI No.

SEÑORA *goes up to Andri and kisses him.*

ANDRI Why did you do that?

SEÑORA I must go.
Noise in the street.
Shall we see each other again?

ANDRI I should like that, Señora.

SEÑORA I always wished I had never known my father and mother.
No one, when he sees the world they have left behind for
him, can understand his parents.
Enter the Teacher and the Mother.
I'm going, yes, I'm just going.
Silence.
So I'll say goodbye.
Silence.
I'm going, yes, now I'm really going . . .
The Señora goes out.

TEACHER Andri, you go with her! But not across the square, take
her round the back way.

ANDRI Why round the back?

TEACHER Just do as I say.
    Andri goes out.
    The Priest will tell him. Don't ask me about it now! I
    never told you, because you've never understood me.
    He sits down.
    Now you know.

MOTHER What will Andri say?

TEACHER He doesn't believe me.
    Noise in the street.
    I hope the mob will leave her alone.

MOTHER I understand more than you think, Can. You loved *her*,
    but you married *me*, because I am an Andorran. You
    have betrayed us all, but Andri more than anyone. Don't
    curse the Andorrans, you are one yourself.
    Enter the Priest.
    You have a difficult task in this house, Reverend Father.
    You explained to Andri what it means to be a Jew and
    that he should accept it. Now he has accepted it. And
    now you must tell him what an Andorran is and that he
    should accept that.

TEACHER Now leave us!

MOTHER May God guide you, Father Benedict.
    The Mother goes out.

PRIEST I tried, but it was no use, it's impossible to talk to them,
    every reasonable word exasperates them. I told them to
    go home and mind their own business. Not one of them
    knows what they really want.
    Andri comes back.

TEACHER Why are you back so soon?

ANDRI She said she wanted to go alone.
    He shows his hand.
    She gave me this.

TEACHER Her ring?

ANDRI Yes.

TEACHER *says nothing, then stands up.*

ANDRI Who is this Señora?

TEACHER I'll go with her.
    The Teacher goes.

PRIEST What are you laughing about?

ANDRI He's jealous!

PRIEST Sit down.

ANDRI What's the matter with you all?

PRIEST It's no laughing matter, Andri.

ANDRI But it's ludicrous.

> *Andri looks at the ring.*

> You know, I think this is a topaz.

PRIEST Andri, we must have a talk.

ANDRI Again?

> *Andri laughs.*

> Everyone is behaving today like puppets when the strings are tangled, including you, Father.

> *Andri takes a cigarette.*

> I believe she was once his mistress.

> *Andri smokes.*

> She's a fantastic woman.

PRIEST Andri, I have something to tell you.

ANDRI Can't I stand while you say it?

> *Andri sits down.*

> I have to be in the shop by two. Isn't she a fantastic woman?

PRIEST I'm glad you like her.

ANDRI Everyone is behaving so strangely.

> *Andri smokes.*

> You're going to tell me that you shouldn't go up to a soldier and knock his cap off when you know you're a Jew, one shouldn't do that at all, and yet I'm glad I did it. I learnt something from it, even if it's no use to me. As a matter of fact not a day passes now, since our talk, without my learning something that is no use to me, Reverend Father, no more use to me than your kind words. I'm sure you mean well, you are a Christian by profession, but I am a Jew by birth, and that's why I am going to emigrate.

PRIEST Andri –

ANDRI If I can.

> *Andri puts out his cigarette.*

I didn't mean to tell anyone that.

PRIEST Stay where you are!

ANDRI This ring will help me.

The Priest says nothing.

Please don't repeat what I've just told you, that's the only thing you can do for me now.

Andri stands up.

I must go.

Andri laughs.

You're quite right, there is something restless about me, Father . . .

PRIEST Are you doing the talking or am I?

ANDRI I'm sorry.

Andri sits down.

I'm listening.

PRIEST Andri –

ANDRI You're so solemn!

PRIEST I have come to redeem you.

ANDRI I'm listening.

PRIEST I knew nothing about it either, Andri, when we talked together last time. For years the story has always been that he rescued a Jewish child, a Christian deed, so why shouldn't I have believed it? But now, Andri, your mother has come –

ANDRI Who has come?

PRIEST The Señora.

ANDRI *jumps up.*

PRIEST Andri – you're not a Jew.

Silence.

Don't you believe me?

ANDRI No.

PRIEST So you think I'm lying?

ANDRI Father, one feels a thing like that.

PRIEST What does one feel?

ANDRI Whether one is a Jew or not.

The Priest stands up and approaches Andri.

Don't touch me! Keep your hands off me! I don't want any more of that.

PRIEST Don't you hear what I say?

ANDRI *says nothing.*

PRIEST You're his son.

ANDRI *laughs.*

PRIEST Andri, that is the truth.

ANDRI How many truths have you got?
Andri takes a cigarette, which he then forgets.
You can't do that with me any more . . .

PRIEST Why don't you believe me?

ANDRI My belief is used up.

PRIEST I swear to you by my soul's salvation, Andri: You are his son, our son, and there can be no question of your being a Jew.

ANDRI There's been plenty of question of it up to now . . .
Noise in the street.

PRIEST What's going on?
Silence.

ANDRI Ever since I have been able to hear, people have told me I'm different, and I watched to see if what they said was true. And it is true, Father: I am different. People told me my kind have a certain way of moving, and I looked at myself in the mirror almost every evening. They are right: I do move like this and like this. I can't help it. And I watched to see whether it was true that I'm always thinking of money, when the Andorrans watch me and think, now he's thinking of money; and they were right again: I am always thinking of money. It's true. And I have no guts, I've tried, it's no use: I have no guts, only fear. And people told me that my kind are cowards. I watched out for this too. Many of them are cowards, but I know when I'm being a coward. I didn't want to admit what they told me, but it's true. They kicked me with their boots, and it's true what they say: I don't feel like they do. And I have no country. You told me, Father, that one must accept that, and I have accepted it. Now it's up to you, Reverend Father, to accept your Jew.

PRIEST Andri –

ANDRI Now, Father, I'm doing the talking.

PRIEST – do you want to be a Jew?

ANDRI I am a Jew. For a long time I didn't know what it meant. Now I know.

PRIEST *sits down helplessly.*

ANDRI I don't want to have a father and mother, for their death to come over me with anguish and despair, nor my death over them. And no sister and no sweetheart. Soon everything will be torn to pieces, then neither our promises nor our fidelity will help. I want it to happen soon. I'm old. My trust has fallen out, one piece after the other, like teeth. I used to be happy, the sun shone green in the trees, I threw my name in the air like a cap that belonged to nobody but me, and down fell a stone that killed me. I have been wrong, all the time, though not in the way they thought. I wanted to be right and to rejoice. But my enemies were right, even if they were unjust, no matter how much I understand I still can't feel that I am right. I don't need enemies any more, the truth is enough. I take fright the moment I begin to hope. I have never been able to hope. I take fright when I laugh, and I can't weep. My affliction raises me above everyone, and therefore I must fall. My eyes are big with melancholy, my blood knows everything, and I wish I were dead. But I have a horror of dying. There is no grace –

PRIEST Now you are committing a sin.

ANDRI Look at the old teacher, the way he is going downhill, and he was once a young man, he says, with great ideals. Look at Barblin. And all of them, all of them, not only me. Look at the soldiers. Damned. Look at yourself. You already know, Father, what you will do when they take me away, a Jew, in front of your kind eyes, and that's why they stare at me so, your kind, kind eyes. You will pray. For me and for yourself. Your prayers won't even help you, you will betray me in spite of them. Grace is an everlasting rumour, the sun will shine green in the trees even when they take me away.

Enter the Teacher, his clothes torn.

PRIEST What has happened?

TEACHER *collapses.*

PRIEST What has happened?

Two men bring in the dead Señora, lay her down and go.

ANDRI The Señora – ?

PRIEST How did that happen?

TEACHER A stone.

PRIEST Who threw it?

TEACHER They say Andri did. The innkeeper saw it with his own eyes.

ANDRI *tries to run out; the Teacher holds him back.*

TEACHER He was here, you are his witness.

FORESTAGE

The Somebody enters the witness box.

SOMEBODY I admit there's no proof as to who threw the stone at the foreign woman that time. I personally wasn't in the square when it happened. I don't want to put the blame on anyone; I'm not the judge of the universe. As to the young lad – of course I remember him. He used to spend all his tips on the juke-box, and when they took him away I felt sorry for him. I don't know what the soldiers did to him after they took him away, we only heard him screaming . . . There must come a time when we are allowed to forget, I think.

10

The square of Andorra. Andri is sitting alone.

ANDRI People are looking at me from all round, I know. Let them look . . .

He takes a cigarette.

I didn't throw the stone!

He smokes.

Let them come out, if they saw it with their own eyes, let them come out of their houses, if they dare, and point their fingers at me.

VOICE *whispers.*

ANDRI Why are you whispering behind the wall?

VOICE *whispers.*

ANDRI I can't hear a word when you whisper.

He smokes.

I've been sitting here for an hour. It's like a dead town. There's no one about. They're all in their cellars. It looks strange. Only the sparrows on the wires.

VOICE *whispers.*

ANDRI Why should I hide?

VOICE *whispers.*

ANDRI I didn't throw the stone.

He smokes.

Since dawn I've been sauntering through your streets. All alone. All the shutters were down, every door shut. There is nothing left but dogs and cats in your snow-white Andorra . . .

The rumbling of a loudspeaker van is heard, loud and reverberating; the words are unintelligible.

You're not supposed to carry a rifle. Did you hear? It's all over.

The Teacher appears, a rifle on his arm.

TEACHER Andri –

ANDRI *smokes.*

TEACHER We've been looking for you all night –

ANDRI Where is Barblin?

TEACHER I was up in the forest –

ANDRI What would I be doing in the forest?

TEACHER Andri – the Blacks are here.

ANDRI Really?

He listens.

TEACHER Listen.

He releases the safety catch of his rifle.

ANDRI Only the sparrows.

The twittering of birds.

TEACHER You can't stay here.

ANDRI Where can I stay?

TEACHER It's senseless, what you're doing, it's madness –
He takes Andri's arm.
Now come along!

ANDRI I didn't throw the stone –
He tears himself away.
I didn't throw the stone!
A sound.

TEACHER What was that?

ANDRI Shutters.
He stamps out his cigarette.
People behind shutters.
He takes another cigarette.
Have you a light?
Drums in the distance.

TEACHER Was that gunfire?

ANDRI It's quieter than it has ever been.

TEACHER What's happening now?

ANDRI The shock of their lives.

TEACHER What did you say?

ANDRI Rather dead than a slave.
Again the rumble of the loudspeaker van.
NO ANDORRAN HAS ANYTHING TO FEAR. Did you hear that?
CALM AND ORDER – ALL BLOODSHED – IN THE NAME OF
PEACE – ANYONE CARRYING OR CONCEALING ARMS – THE
COMMANDER IN CHIEF – NO ANDORRAN HAS ANYTHING TO
FEAR . . .
Silence.
In fact it's exactly what I expected. Exactly.

TEACHER What are you talking about?

ANDRI Your surrender.
Three men without rifles cross the square.
You're the last one with a rifle.

TEACHER Scum!

ANDRI No Andorran has anything to fear.
The twittering of birds.
Haven't you got a light?

TEACHER *stares after the men.*

ANDRI Did you see how they were walking? They didn't look at one another. And they were very quiet! A point comes when everyone realizes how many things he never really believed. That's why they're walking about in that strange way. Like men who have been lying.

Two men without rifles cross the square.

TEACHER My son –

ANDRI Don't start that again!

TEACHER You're lost if you don't believe me.

ANDRI I'm not your son.

TEACHER Andri, no one can choose his father. What else can I do to make you believe me? What else can I do? I tell you at every possible moment. I've even told the children at school that you are my son. What else can I do? Do you want me to hang myself to make you believe it? I'm not leaving you, Andri.

He sits down beside Andri.

Andri –

ANDRI *looks up at the houses.*

A black flag is hoisted.

ANDRI They simply can't wait.

TEACHER Where did they get the flags from?

ANDRI All they need now is a scapegoat.

A second flag is hoisted.

TEACHER Andri, come home!

ANDRI It's no use telling me all over again, Father. Your fate is not mine, Father, nor mine yours.

TEACHER The only witness I had is dead.

ANDRI Don't talk about her!

TEACHER You're wearing her ring –

ANDRI What you have done, no father would do.

TEACHER How can you know?

ANDRI *listens.*

TEACHER An Andorran, they say, has nothing to do with a woman from over the border and certainly doesn't have a child by her. I was afraid of them, yes, afraid of Andorra, because I was a coward –

ANDRI People are listening.

TEACHER That's why I said it – because I was a coward. It was easier, at that time, to have a Jewish child. It was something to be admired. At first they used to fondle you, because it flattered them not to be like the people across the frontier.

ANDRI *listens.*

TEACHER Andri, do you hear your father talking to you?
The sound of a shutter.
Let them listen!
The sound of a shutter.
Andri –

ANDRI They don't believe you.

TEACHER Because you don't believe me!

ANDRI *smokes.*

TEACHER You with your innocence, yes, you didn't throw the stone, say it again, you didn't throw the stone, yes, you with your enormous innocence, look at me like a Jew, but you are my son, yes, my son, and if you don't believe it you are beyond help.

ANDRI I am beyond help.

TEACHER You want me to be guilty!

ANDRI *looks at him.*

TEACHER Go on, say it!

ANDRI What?

TEACHER Tell me to hang myself.
Military music in the distance.

ANDRI They are coming with music.
He takes another cigarette.
I'm not the first one who has been beyond help. There is no point in talking the way you are. I know who my forbears are. Thousands and hundreds of thousands have died at the stake, their fate is mine.

TEACHER Fate!

ANDRI You don't understand that, because you are not a Jew –
He looks into the street.
Now leave me!

ANDRI They're throwing their rifles away.

Enter the Soldier, disarmed and carrying only a drum. The sound of rifles being thrown into a pile can be heard. The Soldier speaks over his shoulder.

SOLDIER But tidily, I said! Like in the Army!
He goes up to the Teacher.
Hand over your rifle.

TEACHER No.

SOLDIER Orders are orders.

TEACHER No.

SOLDIER No Andorran has anything to fear.
Enter the Doctor, the Innkeeper, the Carpenter, the Journeyman, the Somebody, all without rifles.

TEACHER Scum! All of you! Scum! To the last man. Scum!
The Teacher releases the safety catch of his rifle and is about to fire upon the Andorrans, but the Soldier intervenes; after a brief, soundless struggle the Teacher is disarmed and looks round.

TEACHER My son! Where is my son?
The Teacher rushes out.

SOMEBODY What's got into him?
On the forestage right, by the juke-box, Andri appears and drops in a coin so that his tune plays, then slowly walks away.

FORESTAGE

While the juke-box is playing, two soldiers in black uniforms, each carrying a sub-machine gun, march to and fro on sentry-go, passing one another.

11

Outside Barblin's room. Andri and Barblin. Drums in the distance.

ANDRI How often did you sleep with him?

BARBLIN Andri.

ANDRI How often did you sleep with him, while I was sitting
here talking. About going away with you –

BARBLIN *says nothing.*

ANDRI You remember, he stood right here – great hairy chest.

BARBLIN Don't!

ANDRI A real man!

BARBLIN *says nothing.*

ANDRI How often did you sleep with him?

BARBLIN *says nothing.*

ANDRI You don't say anything . . . Then what are we to talk
about all night? I mustn't think about that now, you say.
I should think about my future, but I haven't got a
future, so I should like to know how many times you
slept with him?

BARBLIN *sobs.*

ANDRI And will it carry on?

BARBLIN *sobs.*

ANDRI Why do I want to know anyhow? What's it matter now?
Just to be able to feel something for you again.
Andri listens.

BARBLIN Andri . . .

ANDRI Ssh!

BARBLIN It wasn't like that.

ANDRI I wonder how near they are.

BARBLIN You're not fair.

ANDRI I shall apologize when they come . . .

BARBLIN *sobs.*

ANDRI Why not fair? I thought we loved each other. I'm only
asking what it's like to have a real man. Don't be shy.
Surely you could tell me that, now that you think of
yourself as my little sister.
Andri strokes her hair.
I have waited too long for you.
Andri listens.

BARBLIN They mustn't hurt you!

ANDRI You try and stop them!

BARBLIN I shall stay with you!
Silence.

ANDRI Barblin, now I'm frightened again –

BARBLIN Brother!

ANDRI Suddenly. If they know I'm in the house and they can't find me, they set fire to the house, that's well known, and wait down below till the Jew jumps out of the window.

BARBLIN Andri – you aren't a Jew!

ANDRI Then why do you want to hide me?
Drums in the distance.

BARBLIN Come into my room!

ANDRI *shakes his head.*

BARBLIN Nobody knows there's another room up here.

ANDRI Except Peider.
The drums disappear into the distance.
All wiped out.

BARBLIN What did you say?

ANDRI What is coming has all happened before. I said: All wiped out. My head in your lap. Do you remember? There's no end to it. My head in your lap. Was I in your way? I can't imagine that. So what? I can imagine it. What rubbish did I talk when I wasn't there any more? Why didn't you laugh? You didn't even laugh. All wiped out, all wiped out! And I didn't even feel it when Peider was there, your hair in his hands. So what? It has all happened before . . .
Drums near by.
You see, they know where fear is.

BARBLIN They're going past.

ANDRI They're surrounding the house.
The drums suddenly fall silent.
It's me they're after, you know that very well. I'm not your brother. Lies won't help. There have been too many already.
Silence.
Go on, kiss me!

BARBLIN No.

ANDRI Take your clothes off!

BARBLIN No, Andri.

ANDRI Kiss me, put your arms round me!

BARBLIN *struggles.*

ANDRI What's it matter now?

BARBLIN *struggles.*

ANDRI Don't act so pure, you –
The tinkling of a broken window.

BARBLIN What was that?

ANDRI They know where I am.

BARBLIN Put out the candle!
The tinkling of a second window.

ANDRI Kiss me!

BARBLIN No. No . . .

ANDRI Can't you do with me what you can do with anyone,
merry and naked? I shan't let go of you. Why is it different with others? Go on, tell me. Why is it different?
I shall kiss you, soldier's sweetheart! One more or less,
don't be so fussy. Why is it different with me? Tell me!
Is your hair bored when I kiss it?

BARBLIN Brother –

ANDRI Why do you only feel ashamed with me?

BARBLIN Now let go of me!

ANDRI Now, yes, now and never again, yes, I want you, yes,
merry and naked, yes, little sister, yes, yes, yes –

BARBLIN *screams.*

ANDRI Remember the deadly nightshade.
Andri undoes her blouse as if she were lying unconscious.
Remember our deadly nightshade –

BARBLIN You're out of your mind!
The doorbell rings.
Did you hear that, Andri? You're lost if you don't believe
us. Hide! Hide, Andri!
The doorbell rings.

ANDRI Why didn't we poison ourselves, Barblin, while we were
still children. Now it's too late . . .
Blows on the front door.

BARBLIN Father won't open the door.

ANDRI How slow. How slow they are.
Blows on the front door.

BARBLIN Oh Lord, our God, who art, who art, Lord, Almighty

God, who art in heaven, Lord, Lord, who art – Lord . . .
The front door cracks.

ANDRI Leave me quickly. If they find you with me that won't
be good. Take your blouse. Quickly. Think of your hair.
*Voices in the house. Barblin puts out the candle; the tramp-
ing of boots. The Soldier appears with the drum and two
soldiers in black uniforms equipped with a searchlight: Barblin, without a blouse, alone outside the room.*

SOLDIER Where is he?

BARBLIN Who?

SOLDIER Our Jew.

BARBLIN There isn't any Jew.

SOLDIER *pushes her aside and goes up to the door.*

BARBLIN Don't you dare!

SOLDIER Open up!

BARBLIN Help! Help!

ANDRI *opens the door and steps out.*

SOLDIER That's him.

ANDRI *is bound.*

BARBLIN Don't touch him, he is my brother –

SOLDIER We shall see about that at the Jew Inspection.

BARBLIN The Jew Inspection?

SOLDIER All right, get going.

BARBLIN What's that?

SOLDIER You too. Everybody has to appear at the Jew Inspection.
Come on.
Andri is led away.
Jew's whore!

FORESTAGE

The Doctor enters the witness box.

DOCTOR I shall try to be brief, although there are a great many
things being said today which ought to be corrected. It's
always easy to know afterwards how one ought to have
behaved at the time, quite apart from the fact that as far

as I am personally concerned I really don't know why I should have behaved differently. What did I do? Nothing whatever. I was the local medical officer, as I still am. I can't remember what I am supposed to have said at the time, but anyhow that's my way, an Andorran always says what he thinks – but I must be brief . . . I admit that we were all mistaken at the time, which naturally I can only regret. How often do I have to say that? I'm not in favour of atrocities, I never have been. Anyway, I only saw the young man two or three times. I didn't see the beating-up that is supposed to have taken place later. Nevertheless, I naturally condemn it. I can only say that it's not my fault, quite apart from the fact that his behaviour (there's no point in concealing the fact) became (let us be quite frank) more and more Jewish, although the young man may really have been just as much of an Andorran as I am. I don't for one moment deny that we were somewhat influenced by the events of the period. It was, let us not forget, a turbulent period. As far as I am personally concerned I never took part in brutality or urged anyone to indulge in it. I can state that publicly. A tragic affair, undoubtedly. It wasn't my fault that things turned out as they did. I think I can speak in the name of everyone when, to conclude, I repeat that we can only regret the things that took place at that time.

12

The square of Andorra. The square is surrounded by soldiers in black uniforms, with ordered arms, motionless. The Andorrans, like a herd in the pen, wait mutely to see what is going to happen. For a long time nothing happens. There is only whispering.

DOCTOR Keep calm, everyone. When the Jew Inspection is over everything will remain as before. No Andorran has anything to fear, we've got that in black and white. I shall

remain the medical officer, the innkeeper will remain the
innkeeper, Andorra will remain Andorran . . .
A roll of drums.

JOURNEYMAN Now they're distributing the black cloths.
Black cloths are handed out.

DOCTOR No resistance now, whatever you do.
*Enter Barblin. She goes from group to group as though de-
mented, pulling people's sleeves; they turn their backs on
her; she whispers something that is unintelligible.*

INNKEEPER Now all of a sudden they're saying he isn't one.

SOMEBODY What do they say?

INNKEEPER That he isn't one.

DOCTOR But you can see that he is at a glance.

SOMEBODY Who says that?

INNKEEPER The teacher.

DOCTOR Now we shall see.

INNKEEPER Anyhow he threw the stone.

SOMEBODY Has that been proved?

INNKEEPER Proved?

DOCTOR If he isn't one why is he hiding? Why is he afraid?
Why doesn't he come out into the square like the rest
of us?

INNKEEPER Quite right.

DOCTOR Why shouldn't he be one?

INNKEEPER Quite right.

SOMEBODY They say they've been looking for him all night.

DOCTOR They found him.

SOMEBODY I shouldn't like to be in his shoes.

INNKEEPER Anyhow, he threw the stone –
*They stop talking as a Black soldier approaches; they have
to take the black cloths. The soldier passes on.*

DOCTOR The way they distribute these black cloths without once
raising their voices. That's what I call organization. Just
look at it! That's efficiency!

SOMEBODY They have a smell.
They sniff at their cloths.
The sweat of fear . . .
Barblin comes up to the group containing the Doctor and the

> *Innkeeper, tugs at their sleeves and whispers; they turn their backs on her; she wanders on.*

DOCTOR That's nonsense.

SOMEBODY What did she say?

INNKEEPER She'll pay dearly for that.

DOCTOR No resistance now, whatever you do.

> *Barblin goes up to another group, tugs at their sleeves and whispers; they turn their backs on her; she wanders on.*

INNKEEPER Has it been proved? You ask. When I saw it with my own eyes! Right here on this spot. Who else could have thrown the stone?

SOMEBODY I only asked.

INNKEEPER One of us perhaps?

SOMEBODY I wasn't there.

INNKEEPER But I was!

DOCTOR *puts his finger to his lips.*

INNKEEPER I suppose you think I threw the stone?

DOCTOR Quiet.

INNKEEPER Me?

DOCTOR We're not supposed to talk.

INNKEEPER Here, right here on this spot, the stone was lying here, I saw it myself, a cobble stone, a loose cobble stone, and he picked it up like this –

> *The Innkeeper picks up a cobble stone.*

– just like this . . .

> *The Carpenter joins them.*

CARPENTER What's going on?

DOCTOR Keep calm, keep calm.

CARPENTER What are these black cloths for?

DOCTOR The Jew Inspection.

CARPENTER What are we supposed to do with them?

> *The Black soldiers surrounding the square suddenly present arms: a Black, short, fat, pale, flabby, apparently harmless, crosses the square with brisk, short steps.*

DOCTOR That's him.

CARPENTER Who?

DOCTOR The Jew Detector.

> *The Soldiers order arms with a crash.*

INNKEEPER Suppose he makes a mistake?

DOCTOR He never makes a mistake.

INNKEEPER What would happen?

DOCTOR Why should he make a mistake?

INNKEEPER But just suppose. What would happen?

DOCTOR He has an eye for it. You can be sure of that! He can smell it. He can see it by the walk. If somebody walks across the square, he can see it by the feet.

SOMEBODY Is that why we have to take our shoes off?

DOCTOR He has been trained as a Jew Detector.

Barblin appears again, looking for groups to which she has not yet been. She finds the Journeyman, tugs his sleeve and whispers; the Journeyman pulls himself free.

JOURNEYMAN Leave me alone!

DOCTOR *lights a small cigar.*

JOURNEYMAN She's nuts: she says no one's to walk across the square, we're to let them take us all away. She wants to give us a sign. She's nuts.

A Black soldier sees that the Doctor is smoking and approaches him with fixed bayonet at the ready. The Doctor starts with fright, throws his cigar on the asphalt, stamps it out and turns pale.

They say they have found him . . .

A roll of drums.

This is it.

They put the cloths over their heads.

INNKEEPER I'm not going to put a black cloth over my head!

SOMEBODY Why not?

INNKEEPER I won't do it.

JOURNEYMAN Orders are orders.

INNKEEPER What's the use of it?

DOCTOR They do that wherever one of them has been hiding. That's what you get for it. If we had handed him over straight away –

The Idiot appears.

INNKEEPER Why hasn't he got a black cloth?

SOMEBODY They believe him when he says he isn't one.

The Idiot grins and nods and walks on, scrutinising the

masked people and grinning. Only the Innkeeper is still standing unmasked.

INNKEEPER I won't put a black cloth over my head!

MASKED FIGURE Then he'll be flogged.

INNKEEPER Me?

MASKED FIGURE He hasn't read the yellow poster.

INNKEEPER What do you mean, flogged?

A roll of drums.

MASKED FIGURE This is it.

MASKED FIGURE Keep calm, everyone.

A roll of drums.

INNKEEPER I'm the innkeeper. Why don't you believe me? I'm the innkeeper, everybody knows who I am, I'm the innkeeper, your innkeeper . . .

MASKED FIGURE He's scared!

INNKEEPER Don't you recognize me?

MASKED FIGURE He's scared, he's scared!

Some masked figures laugh.

INNKEEPER I won't put a black cloth over my head . . .

MASKED FIGURE He'll be flogged.

INNKEEPER I'm not a Jew!

MASKED FIGURE He'll be put in a camp.

INNKEEPER I'm not a Jew!

MASKED FIGURE He hasn't read the yellow poster.

INNKEEPER Don't you recognize me? You there! I'm the innkeeper. Who are you? You can't do this to me. You there! I'm the innkeeper, I'm the innkeeper. Surely you recognize me? You can't leave me in the lurch like this. You, Schoolmaster! Who am I?

The Innkeeper has taken hold of the Teacher, who has just appeared with the Mother, unmasked.

TEACHER So it was you who threw the stone, was it?

The Innkeeper drops the cobble stone.

Why do you say my son did it?

The Innkeeper masks himself and mingles with the other masked figures. The Teacher and the Mother stand alone.

That's right, hide under a cloth!

A whistle.

MASKED FIGURE What does that mean?

MASKED FIGURE Shoes off.

MASKED FIGURE Who?

MASKED FIGURE Everyone.

MASKED FIGURE Now?

MASKED FIGURE Shoes off, shoes off.

MASKED FIGURE Why?

MASKED FIGURE He hasn't read the yellow poster . . .

All the masked figures kneel down to take off their shoes. Silence. It takes quite a time.

TEACHER Look at them all on their knees!

A Black soldier comes. The Teacher and the Mother also have to take a black cloth each.

MASKED FIGURE One whistle means shoes off. According to the poster. And two whistles mean march.

MASKED FIGURE Barefoot?

MASKED FIGURE What did he say?

MASKED FIGURE Shoes off, shoes off.

MASKED FIGURE And three whistles means cloth off.

MASKED FIGURE Why cloth off?

MASKED FIGURE All according to the poster.

MASKED FIGURE What did he say?

MASKED FIGURE All according to the poster.

MASKED FIGURE What do two whistles mean?

MASKED FIGURE March?

MASKED FIGURE Why barefoot?

MASKED FIGURE And three whistles mean cloth off.

MASKED FIGURE Where are we to put our shoes?

MASKED FIGURE Why cloth off?

MASKED FIGURE Where are we to put our shoes?

MASKED FIGURE Cloth off means he's found the Jew.

MASKED FIGURE All according to the poster.

MASKED FIGURE No Andorran has anything to fear.

MASKED FIGURE What did he say?

MASKED FIGURE No Andorran has anything to fear.

MASKED FIGURE Where are we to put our shoes?

The Teacher, unmasked, walks in among the masked figures and is the only one standing up.

TEACHER Andri is my son.

MASKED FIGURE That's not our fault!

TEACHER Do you hear what I say?

MASKED FIGURE What did he say?

MASKED FIGURE He says Andri is his son.

MASKED FIGURE Then why is he hiding?

TEACHER I say Andri is my son.

MASKED FIGURE Anyhow, he threw the stone.

TEACHER Which of you says that?

MASKED FIGURE Where are we to put our shoes?

TEACHER Why do you lie? One of you did it. Why do you say my son did it –

A roll of drums.

You don't want to know the truth. Cover it up with a cloth! You don't want to know. Cover it up with a cloth! You'll still have your murderer serving you. What does it matter, so long as the innkeeper is still the innkeeper, the doctor still the medical officer. Just look at them! See the way they put out their shoes in a line. All according to the poster! And one of them is a murderer. Cover it up with a cloth! They only hate the one who reminds them of it –

A roll of drums.

What a people you are! God in heaven, who fortunately for you doesn't exist, what a people you are!

Enter the Soldier with the drum.

SOLDIER Ready? On your feet! Everybody over there! Take your shoes.

All the masked figures stand up with their shoes in their hands.

Put your shoes on the ground. But tidily. Like in the Army. Understand? Shoe next to shoe. Got it? The Army is responsible for law and order. And no answering back.

The Soldier examines the row of shoes.

I said shoe next to shoe. What sort of impression is that going to make?

MASKED FIGURE I'm the innkeeper.

SOLDIER Too far back!

The masked figure straightens out his shoes.

Right, everybody over there at the double. I shall read
out the order again.

Quiet.

'Citizens of Andorra! The Jew Inspection is a measure for
the protection of the population in liberated areas, and for
the restoration of law and order. No Andorran has anything to fear. For instructions see yellow poster.' Quiet!
'Andorra, 15th September, Commander-in-Chief.' –
Why haven't you got a cloth over your head?

TEACHER Where is Andri? Where is my son?

SOLDIER He's here, don't worry, he didn't slip through our fingers.
He'll march. Barefoot like everyone else.

TEACHER Andri is my son.

SOLDIER We shall soon see about that –

A roll of drums.

Get back! Dress by the right! Close up!

The masked figures form up.

All right then, citizens of Andorra, do you understand?
Not a word is to be spoken when the Jew Detector is
here. Is that clear? Everything must be done right, that's
important. When the Jew Detector whistles, stop immediately. Understand? You're not expected to come to
attention. Is that clear? Only the Army comes to attention, because they have practised it. Anyone who is not
a Jew will be free to go. That is to say, you will go straight
back to work. I shall beat the drum.

The Soldier does so.

Then you will walk forward one after the other. Anyone
who doesn't stop when the Jew Detector whistles will be
shot out of hand. Is that clear?

The ringing of a bell.

TEACHER Why isn't the priest here?

SOLDIER He'll be praying for the Jew!

TEACHER The priest knows the truth –

Enter the Jew Detector.

SOLDIER Silence!

*The Black soldiers present arms and stand rigidly in this
position until the Jew Detector, who behaves like a simple
official, has sat down in the armchair in the centre of the
square. The soldiers then order arms. The Jew Detector
takes off his pince-nez, polishes them, puts them on again.
The Teacher and the Mother are now also masked. The
Jew Detector waits until the bell has stopped ringing, then he
gives a sign and two blasts are blown on a whistle.*

SOLDIER First one!
Nobody moves.
Come on, come on!
The Idiot is the first to move.
Not you!
Nervous laughter among the masked figures.
Silence!
A drumbeat.
What's the matter, damn you? All you've got to do is
walk across the square.
No one moves.
No Andorran has anything to fear . . .
Barblin, masked, steps forward.
Come on!
*Barblin goes up to the Jew Detector and throws the black
cloth down at his boots.*
Hey, what's the idea?

BARBLIN This is the sign.
Movement among the masked figures.
Tell him, no Andorran will cross the square! Not one of
us! Then let them flog us! Tell him! Then let them shoot
us all!
*Two Black soldiers seize Barblin, who struggles in vain.
No one moves. The Black soldiers all round have brought
their guns into the firing position. All without a sound.
Barblin is dragged away.*

SOLDIER . . . All right, now get moving. One after the other. Have
we got to flog you? Come on, next one. One after the
other.
Now they start walking.

Slowly, slowly! Next one!
Those who have gone past remove the cloths from their heads.
The cloths are to be folded up. But tidily, I said. Is this
country a pigsty? The national emblem must be in the
top right-hand corner. What will our foreign friends
think of us?
Others walk too slowly.
Get a move on, can't you.
*The Jew Detector studies their walk carefully, but with the
casualness of habit and bored by his own self-confidence.
One figure trips over the cobble stone.*
Just look at that!

MASKED FIGURE My name is Prader.

SOLDIER Come on.

MASKED FIGURE Who tripped me up?

SOLDIER Nobody tripped you up.
The Carpenter takes off his cloth.

SOLDIER Come on, I said, come on. The next. And those who have
gone past are to take their shoes at once. Do I have to
tell you everything, God damn it? Is this a kindergarten?

CARPENTER Somebody tripped me up.

SOLDIER Silence!
One figure goes in the wrong direction.
You're like a bunch of chickens!
A few who have already gone past giggle.

MASKED FIGURE I'm the medical officer.

SOLDIER All right, all right.

DOCTOR *takes off his cloth.*

SOLDIER Take your shoes.

DOCTOR I can't see when I have a cloth over my head. I'm not
used to it. How can I walk when I can't see the ground?

SOLDIER Come on, I said, come on.

DOCTOR It's an impertinence!

SOLDIER The next.
Drumbeat.
Can't you put your damn shoes on at home? I told you,
those who have been passed are to take their shoes and go.
What are you standing around gawping for?

> *Drumbeat.*
> Next.

DOCTOR Where are my shoes? Somebody has taken my shoes. Those aren't my shoes.

SOLDIER Why pick on that pair?

DOCTOR They are standing in my place.

SOLDIER You really are like a lot of kids!

DOCTOR Well, are those my shoes?

> *Drumbeat.*
> I'm not going without my shoes.

SOLDIER Don't start kicking up a fuss!

DOCTOR I'm not going barefoot. I'm not used to it. And speak properly to me, I won't be spoken to in that tone.

SOLDIER Well, what's the matter with you?

DOCTOR I'm not kicking up a fuss.

SOLDIER What the hell do you want?

DOCTOR My shoes.

> *The Jew Detector gives a sign. A blast is blown on the whistle.*

SOLDIER I'm on duty!

> *Drumbeat.*
> Next.
> *No one moves.*

DOCTOR Those aren't my shoes!

SOLDIER *takes the shoes from his hand.*

DOCTOR I shall lodge a complaint, yes, I shall lodge a complaint, someone has moved my shoes, I shan't budge a step, and certainly not if I'm shouted at.

SOLDIER Who do these shoes belong to?

DOCTOR They're not mine –

SOLDIER Who do these shoes belong to?

> *He puts them down at the front by the footlights.*
> We shall see!

DOCTOR I know very well who they belong to.

SOLDIER Get a move on!

> *Drumbeat.*
> Next.
> *No one moves.*

DOCTOR Here they are!
No one moves.

SOLDIER Scared again, are we? Come on!
Once more they go one after the other. The procedure has become automatic so that it is now tedious. One of those who has walked past the Jew Detector and now takes the cloth from his head is the Journeyman.

JOURNEYMAN What was that about the national emblem?

SOMEONE Top right-hand corner.

JOURNEYMAN Has he been through yet?
The Jew Detector gives a sign. Three blasts are blown on the whistle.

SOLDIER Stop!
The masked figure stands still.
Off with your cloth!
The masked figure doesn't move.
Off with your cloth, Jew, do you hear!
The Soldier goes up to the masked figure and takes off his cloth. It is the Somebody, rigid with terror.
That's not him. He only looks like that because he's scared. It's not him. There's nothing to be scared about, man! He looks quite different when he's happy . . .
The Jew Detector has risen, walks round the Somebody and scrutinizes him for a long time like an indifferent but conscientious official. The Somebody's appearance visibly changes. The Jew Detector holds his ballpoint pen under the Somebody's chin.

SOLDIER Head up, man. Don't stare down at the ground like one of them!
The Jew Detector also studies his feet, sits down again and gives a negligent sign.
Clear off!
Tension relaxes in the crowd.

DOCTOR He doesn't make mistakes. What did I say? He doesn't make mistakes, he has an eye for it . . .
Drumbeat.

SOLDIER Next.
They start walking again in single file.

What sort of filthy behaviour is that? Can't you use your
own handkerchief when you sweat? Whatever next!
A masked figure picks up the cobble-stone.
What do you think you're doing?

MASKED FIGURE I'm the innkeeper –

SOLDIER What are you messing about with that stone for?

MASKED FIGURE I'm the innkeeper – I – I –
The Innkeeper remains masked.

SOLDIER That's no reason to wet yourself!
There are giggles here and there, as people giggle over a well-liked but ridiculous figure; in the midst of this nervous hilarity come three blasts on the whistle, following a sign from the Jew Detector.

SOLDIER Stop. –
The Teacher takes off his cloth.
Not you, that one there, the other one!
The masked figure does not move.
Off with your cloth!
The Jew Detector stands up.

DOCTOR He has an eye for it. What did I say? He can see by the
walk . . .

SOLDIER Three paces forward!

DOCTOR He's got him . . .

SOLDIER Three paces back!
The masked figure obeys.
Laugh!

DOCTOR He can tell by the laugh . . .

SOLDIER Laugh, or they'll fire.
The masked figure tries to laugh.
Louder!
The masked figure tries to laugh.

DOCTOR That's a Jew's laugh . . .
The Soldier pushes the masked figure.

SOLDIER Off with your cloth, Jew, there's no help for you. Off
with your cloth. Show your face. Or they'll fire.

TEACHER Andri!

SOLDIER I shall count three.
The masked figure does not move.

One –

TEACHER No!

SOLDIER Two –

The Teacher pulls off the figure's cloth.

Three . . .

TEACHER My son!

The Jew Detector walks round Andri, examining him.

He is my son!

The Jew Detector examines Andri's feet, then gives a sign, just as negligently as before but a different sign, and two Black soldiers take charge of Andri.

CARPENTER Let's go.

MOTHER *steps forward and takes off her cloth.* No!

SOLDIER What the hell do you want?

MOTHER I shall tell the truth.

SOLDIER Is Andri your son?

MOTHER No.

SOLDIER Did you hear that! Did you hear that!

MOTHER But Andri is my husband's son –

INNKEEPER Let her prove it.

MOTHER It's true. And Andri didn't throw the stone, I know that too, because he was at home when it happened. I swear to that. I was at home myself. I know that and I swear it by Almighty God who is our judge in eternity.

INNKEEPER She's lying.

MOTHER It's true! Let him go!

The Jew Detector stands up again.

SOLDIER Silence!

The Jew Detector goes up to Andri and repeats the examination, then he empties out Andri's trouser pockets; coins fall out; the Andorrans recoil from the rolling money as though it were lava; the Soldier laughs.

Jew money.

DOCTOR He doesn't make mistakes . . .

TEACHER What do you mean, Jew money? It's your money, our money. What else have you got in your own pockets?

The Jew Detector feels Andri's hair.

Andri, why don't you speak?

ANDRI *smiles.*

TEACHER He is my son, he mustn't die, my son, my son!
The Jew Detector leaves; the Blacks present arms; the Soldier takes charge.

SOLDIER Where did you get that ring?

CARPENTER He has got valuables too . . .

SOLDIER Give it here!

ANDRI No.

SOLDIER Come on, hand it over!

ANDRI No – please . . .

SOLDIER Or they'll hack your finger off.

ANDRI No! No!
Andri struggles.

CARPENTER Look how he fights for his valuables . . .

DOCTOR Let's go . . .
Andri is surrounded by Black soldiers and out of sight when he gives vent to a scream; then silence. Andri is led away.

TEACHER That's it. Slink away to your homes – You didn't see it, you know nothing – go home and look at yourselves in your mirrors and be sick, be sick.
The Andorrans disappear in all directions, everyone taking his shoes.

SOLDIER He won't be needing shoes any more.
The Soldier goes.

SOMEBODY The poor Jew –

INNKEEPER What can we do about it.

CARPENTER I could do with a brandy. That business with the finger was going too far . . .

DOCTOR I could do with a brandy myself.

CARPENTER His shoes are still there.

DOCTOR Let's go inside.

CARPENTER That business with the finger was going too far . . .
The Carpenter, the Doctor and the Innkeeper disappear into the inn. The stage grows dark; the juke-box begins to play of its own accord, the same record. When the stage lights up again, Barblin is on her knees whitewashing the asphalt of the square; her head has been shaved. Enter the Priest. The music stops.

BARBLIN I'm whitewashing, I'm whitewashing.

PRIEST Barblin!

BARBLIN Why shouldn't I whitewash my father's house, Reverend Father?

PRIEST You're talking wildly.

BARBLIN I'm whitewashing.

PRIEST That isn't your father's house, Barblin.

BARBLIN I'm whitewashing, I'm whitewashing.

PRIEST There's no sense in it.

BARBLIN There's no sense in it.

Enter the Innkeeper.

INNKEEPER What is she doing?

BARBLIN There are his shoes.

INNKEEPER *is about to fetch the shoes.*

BARBLIN Don't touch them!

PRIEST She has lost her reason.

BARBLIN I'm whitewashing, I'm whitewashing. What are you doing? If you can't see what I see, then you can see what I'm doing – I'm whitewashing.

INNKEEPER Stop that!

BARBLIN Blood, blood, blood everywhere.

INNKEEPER Those are my tables!

BARBLIN My tables, your tables, our tables.

INNKEEPER Make her stop it!

BARBLIN Who are you?

PRIEST I've tried everything.

BARBLIN I'm whitewashing, I'm whitewashing, so that we shall have a white Andorra, you murderers, a snow-white Andorra; I shall whitewash all of you, all of you.

Enter the former Soldier.

Tell him to leave me alone, Father, he has his eye on me, Father, I'm engaged.

SOLDIER I'm thirsty.

BARBLIN He doesn't know me.

SOLDIER Who is she?

BARBLIN The Jew's whore, Barblin.

SOLDIER Go away!

BARBLIN Who are you?

Barblin laughs.

Where has your drum got to?

SOLDIER Stop laughing!

BARBLIN Where have you taken my brother?

Enter the Carpenter.

Where have you come from, all of you? Where are you going to, all of you? Why don't you go home, all of you, all of you, and hang yourselves?

CARPENTER What did she say?

BARBLIN Him too!

INNKEEPER She's off her rocker.

SOLDIER Get rid of her.

BARBLIN I'm whitewashing.

CARPENTER What's the idea of that?

BARBLIN I'm whitewashing, I'm whitewashing.

Enter the Doctor.

Have you seen a finger?

DOCTOR *speechless.*

BARBLIN Haven't you seen a finger?

SOLDIER That's enough of that!

PRIEST Leave her alone.

INNKEEPER She's a public nuisance.

CARPENTER Tell her to leave us alone.

INNKEEPER What can we do about it?

JOURNEYMAN I warned her.

DOCTOR The proper place for her is a lunatic asylum.

BARBLIN *stares.*

PRIEST Her father has hanged himself in the schoolroom. She is looking for her father, she is looking for her hair, she is looking for her brother.

All, apart from the Priest and Barblin, go into the inn.

Barblin, do you hear who is speaking to you?

BARBLIN *whitewashes the asphalt.*

PRIEST I've come to take you home.

BARBLIN I'm whitewashing.

PRIEST I'm Father Benedict.

BARBLIN *whitewashes the asphalt.*

PRIEST I'm Father Benedict.

BARBLIN Where were you, Father Benedict, when they took away our brother like a beast to the slaughter, like a beast to the slaughter, where were you? You have turned black, Father Benedict . . .

PRIEST *says nothing.*

BARBLIN Father is dead.

PRIEST I know, Barblin.

BARBLIN And my brother?

PRIEST I pray for Andri every day.

BARBLIN And my hair?

PRIEST Your hair, Barblin, will grow again –

BARBLIN Like the grass out of the graves.

The Priest starts to lead Barblin away, but she suddenly stops and turns back to the shoes.

PRIEST Barblin – Barblin . . .

BARBLIN Those are his shoes. Don't touch them. When he comes back, those are his shoes.

Curtain.

The Master Playwrights

Collections of plays by the best-known modern playwrights in value-for money paperbacks.

John Arden	PLAYS: ONE *Serjeant Musgrave's Dance, The Workhouse Donkey, Armstrong's Last Goodnight*
Brendan Behan	THE COMPLETE PLAYS *The Hostage, The Quare Fellow, Richard's Cork Leg, Moving Out, A Garden Party, The Big House*
Edward Bond	PLAYS: ONE *Saved, Early Morning, The Pope's Wedding* PLAYS: TWO *Lear, The Sea, Narrow Road to the Deep North, Black Mass, Passion*
Noël Coward	PLAYS: ONE *Hay Fever, The Vortex, Fallen Angels, Easy Virtue* PLAYS: TWO *Private Lives, Bitter Sweet, The Marquise, Post-Mortem* PLAYS: THREE *Design for Living, Cavalcade, Conversation Piece,* and *Hands Across the Sea, Still Life* and *Fumed Oak* from *Tonight at 8.30* PLAYS: FOUR *Blithe Spirit, This Happy Breed, Present Laughter,* and *Ways and Means, The Astonished Heart* and *Red Peppers* from *Tonight at 8.30* PLAYS: FIVE *Relative Values, Look After Lulu, Waiting in the Wings, Suite in Three Keys*
Henrik Ibsen	*Translated and introduced by Michael Meyer* PLAYS: ONE *Ghosts, The Wild Duck, The Master Builder* PLAYS: TWO *A Doll's House, An Enemy of the People, Hedda Gabler* PLAYS: THREE *Rosmersholm, Little Eyolf, The Lady from the Sea* PLAYS: FOUR *John Gabriel Borkman, The Pillars of Society, When We Dead Awaken*